A gift from:
Friends of the
Pinole Library

EXPLORERS
AND
EXPLORATION

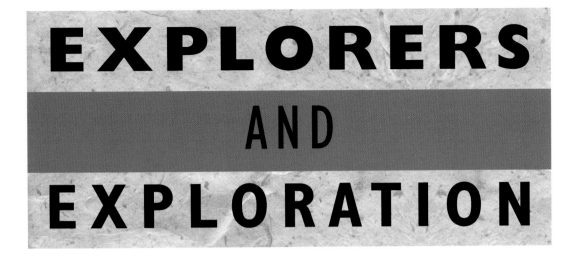

3

CHENG HO – ELLSWORTH, LINCOLN

Marshall Cavendish
New York • London • Singapore

Marshall Cavendish
99 White Plains Road
Tarrytown, New York 10591-9001

www.marshallcavendish.com

Consultants: Ralph Ehrenberg, former chief, Geography and Map Division, Library of Congress, Washington, DC; Conrad Heidenreich, former historical geography professor, York University, Toronto; Shane Winser, information officer, Royal Geographical Society, London

Contributing authors: Dale Anderson, Kay Barnham, Peter Chrisp, Richard Dargie, Paul Dowswell, Elizabeth Gogerly, Steven Maddocks, John Malam, Stewart Ross, Shane Winser

MARSHALL CAVENDISH
Editor: Thomas McCarthy
Editorial Director: Paul Bernabeo
Production Manager: Michael Esposito

WHITE-THOMSON PUBLISHING
Editors: Alex Woolf and Steven Maddocks
Design: Derek Lee and Ross George
Cartographer: Peter Bull Design
Picture Research: Glass Onion Pictures
Indexer: Fiona Barr

ISBN 0-7614-7535-4 (set)
ISBN 0-7614-7538-9 (vol. 3)

Printed in China

08 07 06 05 04 5 4 3 2 1

Library of Congress Cataloging-in-Publication Data

Explorers and exploration.
   p. cm.
  Includes bibliographical references (p.   ) and index.
  ISBN 0-7614-7535-4 (set : alk. paper) -- ISBN 0-7614-7536-2 (v. 1) -- ISBN 0-7614-7537-0 (v. 2) -- ISBN 0-7614-7538-9 (v. 3) -- ISBN 0-7614-7539-7 (v. 4) -- ISBN 0-7614-7540-0 (v. 5) -- ISBN 0-7614-7541-9 (v. 6) -- ISBN 0-7614-7542-7 (v. 7) -- ISBN 0-7614-7543-5 (v. 8) -- ISBN 0-7614-7544-3 (v. 9) -- ISBN 0-7614-7545-1 (v. 10) -- ISBN 0-7614-7546-X (v. 11)
  1. Explorers--Encyclopedias. 2. Discoveries in geography--Encyclopedias. I. Marshall Cavendish Corporation. II. Title.
  G80.E95 2005
  910'.92'2--dc22

          2004048292

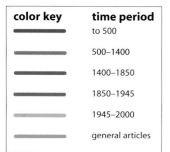

color key	time period
▬▬▬	to 500
▬▬▬	500–1400
▬▬▬	1400–1850
▬▬▬	1850–1945
▬▬▬	1945–2000
▬▬▬	general articles

Exploration during the Ming Dynasty

The Ming dynasty was a family of emperors that ruled China from 1368 to 1644. At the time of Cheng Ho's naval expeditions (1405–1433), Chinese shipbuilding and navigation were far in advance of the rest of the world's. Some of the larger Chinese vessels were capable of carrying hundreds of men or thousands of tons of goods.

However, Ming emperors disagreed over how their wealth should be spent. After Cheng Ho's final expedition, a decision was made to divert money away from seafaring and toward the defense of China's western borders. To make sure that this decision was not overturned, larger ships were destroyed—as were many of the records of Cheng Ho's travels.

Below **The Chinese emperor Chu Ti, shown here being ceremonially borne by servants, was born in 1360 and ruled from 1402 until his death in 1424.**

However, after only one year as emperor, Chu Kao-chih died and was succeeded by his son. The new emperor, Chu Chan-chi, restored his grandfather's program of exploration. In 1430 he ordered the treasure fleet to embark on another voyage, and the following year it set sail for the seventh time. Cheng Ho again commanded the voyage, which proved to be his last. He died in Calicut, on the west coast of India, in 1435.

After Cheng Ho's death, a political struggle in China resulted in a new law that prohibited the construction of vessels with more than three masts. The era of the treasure fleet and of China's naval expeditions was over, and the stage was set for the Europeans to take control of the East Asian trade routes.

SEE ALSO

- Navigation
- Shipbuilding

c. 1371
Cheng Ho is born in Yunnan Province.

1384
Is chosen for imperial service.

1402
Prince Chu Ti seizes the throne.

1405–1407
Cheng Ho's first voyage sails by way of Vietnam to Sumatra.

1407–1409
Second voyage reaches Calicut on the western coast of India.

1409–1411
Third voyage reaches Ceylon (present-day Sri Lanka).

1413–1415
Fourth voyage reaches the Persian Gulf.

1417–1419
Fifth voyage reaches the east coast of Africa and Mozambique Channel.

1421–1422
Sixth voyage makes further exploration of the East African coast.

1424
The emperor dies, and his successor, Chu Kao-chih, halts expeditions and shipbuilding.

1426
A new emperor, Chu Chan-chi, orders the treasure fleet expeditions to begin again.

1431–1433
During his seventh voyage, Cheng Ho visits Southeast Asia, India, and Persia.

1435
Cheng Ho dies in Calicut.

CHRONOMETER

A CHRONOMETER IS a clock that measures time with great accuracy. *Chronometer* comes from two Greek words: *chronos* (time) and *metron* (measure). The first chronometers were built in the eighteenth century by the English inventor John Harrison in order to determine a ship's longitude (its position east or west of an imaginary line running from the North to the South Pole).

Below **Sitting in front of his earlier and much larger sea clocks, John Harrison holds his chronometer.**

THE LONGITUDE PROBLEM

Before John Harrison invented the chronometer, navigators had no sure way of calculating longitude. To keep track of their ship's speed and direction, sailors relied on a method known as dead reckoning, which was often inaccurate. In 1707 a mistaken reckoning led to the death of two thousand English sailors when their fleet was wrecked off the Scilly Isles. After this disaster the government offered the huge sum of £20,000 (worth at least a million dollars now) to anyone who could solve the longitude problem.

On a globe longitude is represented by meridians, 360 imaginary lines that run from Pole to Pole and divide the earth into degrees. Longitude is measured in degrees east or west from a given zero meridian. The English chose to use the meridian running through Greenwich in London for this purpose.

For every fifteen degrees traveled east or west, there is a time difference of one hour. Therefore, the longitude of any location can be worked out from the precise local time. So the obvious answer to the longitude problem was to build an accurate clock. With an accu-

---

1735
John Harrison builds his first sea clock, H1.

1741
Harrison completes H2 but is not satisfied with it.

1757
Harrison finishes H3, another large clock, but decides to produce a small pocket-sized chronometer instead.

1759
Harrison completes H4.

1761
H4 keeps excellent time on a voyage to Jamaica, yet Harrison is awarded only half the prize money.

1772
Captain Cook sails to the Pacific with K1, a version of H4 that could be mass-produced.

1773
After the king intervenes on Harrison's behalf, Harrison is awarded the rest of the prize money.

CONTENTS

CHENG HO

CHENG HO, whose name is also spelled Zheng He, was born around 1371 and died in 1435. One of China's most famous navigators, Cheng Ho led seven pioneering maritime expeditions across and beyond the Indian Ocean between the years 1405 and 1433.

RISE TO PROMINENCE

Cheng Ho was brought up as a Muslim in Yunnan (in present-day southern China). His original name was Ma San-pao, but he was known more familiarly as Ma Ho. During the latter part of the fourteenth century, Yunnan was annexed by China, which was ruled at that time by the Ming dynasty (1368–1644). The Chinese considered Muslims rebels and

at age ten, Ma Ho was captured, castrated, and forced to serve in the Chinese army.

Despite the dreadful treatment he had received, Ma Ho soon gained a reputation as a brave and popular soldier. He was employed by Prince Chu Ti, the emperor's uncle, first as a servant and then as an officer.

In 1402 the prince seized the throne and became emperor himself. He showed his grat-

Below **This sixteenth-century Chinese junk is similar to ships that were built during Cheng Ho's lifetime.**

rate clock the time at Greenwich could be compared with the local time—calculated from the height of the sun, usually at noon.

In the eighteenth century few people thought that such an accurate clock could be built. It was difficult enough for clocks to keep accurate time on land. Yet at sea they had to cope with the rolling of the ship and extreme changes of temperature and humidity. On a long voyage a clock might have to keep time for many months.

HARRISON'S SEA CLOCKS

John Harrison set to work on the longitude problem in 1727. By 1735 he had built his first "sea clock," now called H1. Housed in a four-foot-square (900 cm²) box, it was driven by springs and counterbalances that compensated for the rolling sea. H1 was a great achievement, yet Harrison was not satisfied with its timekeeping.

It was only with his fourth chronometer, H4, finished in 1759, that Harrison produced a timepiece accurate enough to win the longitude prize. Unlike his earlier bulky clocks, H4, five inches (12.5 cm) in diameter, resembled a large pocket watch. When H4 was tested in 1761 on a run of ten weeks from Britain to Jamaica, it lost only five seconds, well within the thirty seconds allowed by the competition rules. In 1772 James Cook took a copy of H4 on his second Pacific voyage. Cook was delighted with the chronometer and described it as "our trusty friend the Watch."

Harrison's chronometer was too expensive to be mass-produced for ships' captains. However, detailed plans were given to the clock maker Larcum Kendall, who solved the production problems. By 1860 the British Royal Navy, which had two hundred ships, owned eight hundred chronometers. Their use allowed explorers to produce accurate maps of their discoveries and also saved the lives of countless sailors.

John Harrison 1693–1776

John Harrison was the son of a Yorkshire carpenter. Although he was expected to follow his father's trade, Harrison's real interest was in clocks, which he taught himself to repair and to make—at first entirely out of wood. In 1727 Harrison began work on his chronometers, a task that would occupy him for the rest of his life. Building the chronometer was less of a problem than convincing the Board of Longitude that he deserved to win the prize. Although his fourth chronometer passed the test in 1761, Harrison did not receive the complete prize money for another twelve years.

Below A leading British watchmaker, Larcum Kendall, produced a copy of Harrison's H4, known as K1. James Cook took K1, which resembled a large pocket watch, on his second Pacific voyage and described it as his "never failing guide."

SEE ALSO

CLOTHING

PEOPLE AROUND THE WORLD wear clothing suited to their local climate. For explorers the correct clothing can mean the difference between the success and failure of an expedition. In extreme circumstances, clothing becomes a matter of life and death.

Right **Some items of clothing worn by Robert F. Scott on his 1901–1904 Antarctic expedition.**

The development of artificial fabrics in modern times has greatly improved the performance of outdoor clothing. Lightweight garments can now be made to withstand extreme weather conditions. There are fabrics that keep water out while allowing perspiration to escape and fabrics that keep the body warm in subzero temperatures or cool in the searing heat of the sun. Many fabrics are designed to allow freedom of movement, an important feature for explorers traveling in difficult terrain.

EXPLORERS IN FREEZING CLIMATES

In the Arctic, blizzards appear out of nowhere, and the wind is bitter and relentless. Snow can be deep and difficult to walk through and often hides dangerous crevasses. Temperatures that can dip well below zero weaken a person's ability to think and to survive. Thus, it is vital that explorers keep warm and dry and protect themselves from the wind.

At the beginning of the twentieth century, wool and heavy canvas jackets were commonly worn by explorers venturing into polar regions. Boots made of leather and gloves made of fur provided only poor insulation from the cold, and as a result, many polar explorers suffered the crippling effects of

frostbite. The lack of suitable protection for eyes from the brightness of the snow led in many cases to snow blindness.

By the latter part of the twentieth century, polar and mountain explorers were wearing a

Above **On a 1990 walk to the North Pole, this explorer wears technologically advanced fabrics designed to protect him from the wind and cold.**

The Race to the Pole

*I*n late 1911 the Norwegian explorer Roald Amundsen (1872–1928) and the British explorer Robert Falcon Scott (1868–1912) both set off on a long, cold Antarctic journey, each aiming to be the first to reach the South Pole. One of the many reasons why Amundsen won the race had to do with the type of clothing used by his team. As well as light, windproof suits, the Norwegians wore suits made of wolf skin fur similar to those worn by the Inuit people.

Meanwhile, Scott's men wore mainly woolen clothes—including woolen underwear—with cotton gabardine topcoats. The woolen clothing did not perform well in subzero temperatures. When wet it was heavy, chafed against the skin, and offered little protection from the wind. Similarly, the cotton gabardine coats were not nearly as efficient as Amundsen's fur suits. Consequently, Scott and his team suffered from frostbite, which slowed them down and ultimately contributed to their death.

combination of lightweight garments to achieve a high standard of protection against the climate. A typical outfit could include several layers of clothing. Such outfits guarantee the warmth of the wearer by trapping several insulating layers of air around the body. During heavy work, on the other hand, the explorer may remove layers to avoid overheating. Other late-twentieth-century innovations included sunblock of a very high SPF (sun protection factor) and goggles that shield the eyes from the sun's ultraviolet rays.

EXPLORERS IN DESERT CLIMATES

Deserts—vast barren areas with little or no water or vegetation—present entirely different dangers to those that travel through them. Cloudless skies make deserts baking hot in the daytime but freezing cold at night, and desert clothing must protect the wearer from both extremes of temperature.

Travelers in desert regions must stay cool during the day so that they sweat less and thus preserve the body's precious reserves of water. Desert clothing must also protect the wearer from the damaging rays of the sun and from dust blown up by the wind. Traditional desert dwellers wear loose garments, head coverings, and sandals. Modern travelers in desert regions wear very similar clothing. A hat with a wide brim keeps the head and the back of the neck shaded. Sunglasses protect the eyes from exposure to to the sun's harmful rays. Loose-fitting, long-sleeved shirts and long pants made from natural fabrics allow air to circulate freely over the skin and thus keep the body temperature low. Finally, boots with thick soles protect feet from the hot desert sand and from spiky vegetation.

EXPLORERS AT SEA

Paintings of explorers from the early modern period indicate that they chose their clothing according to the fashions of the time rather than the specific requirements of life on board a ship. A portrait of Sir Martin Frobisher, the sixteenth-century English navigator, shows him wearing a ruff, doublet, loose knee-length pants, hose, and flimsy leather shoes. Even an ordinary sailor from the same period is shown wearing a shirt, enormous loose pants, and a full-length coat. Such clothes as these would not have served to protect the wearer very well from stormy weather and high seas.

Modern sailors take advantage of high-performance clothing that keeps them dry yet lets perspiration out. For lone sailors on small yachts, it is important that clothes allow the body to breathe, as the same outfit is usually

Charles Macintosh *1766–1843*

Charles Macintosh (after whom the mackintosh raincoat is named) was a Scottish chemist best known for inventing a type of waterproofing. While experimenting with waste products from Glasgow's gasworks, he discovered that India rubber dissolved when it came into contact with coal-tar naphtha. By sandwiching this mixture between two pieces of wool cloth, Macintosh created a waterproof fabric. He patented this fabric in 1823 and worked with Thomas Hancock (1786–1865), an English inventor, to manufacture waterproof clothing. A drawback of early waterproof garments was that rain seeped in through the tiny holes made by a needle when the fabric was sewn together. Temperature also affected the garments: they became very sticky when it was hot and stiff when it was cold. In 1839, when a more temperature-tolerant vulcanized rubber was developed, the manufacture of truly waterproof clothing became possible.

worn for long periods. Sailing boots are waterproof and have nonslip soles.

In Arctic and Antarctic waters, sailors wear an immersion suit in case they are swept overboard. The seas are so cold that just a few minutes spent in the water can cause hypothermia and lead to death. An immersion suit is designed to protect wearers against the cold while a life preserver keeps them afloat.

Underwater Exploration

The first underwater swimmers dived without special clothing or equipment; they simply held their breath. Such divers were unable, however, to go very deep. In order to explore the ocean depths more fully, divers needed an adequate air supply and special clothing to keep them warm once they reached depths beyond the reach of the sun's rays. Two twentieth-century inventions greatly enhanced underwater exploration: the Aqua-Lung allows divers to breathe underwater, and the wet suit prevents the body temperature from dropping dangerously low. Wet suits, constructed of a man-made rubber called neoprene, are designed to trap a thin layer of water next to the wearer's skin. This water is heated by the diver's body and thus provides an insulating layer that keeps the body warm. Dry suits are lined with a waterproof material that keeps the diver completely dry and warm in cold water.

The deeper a diver goes, the greater the water pressure he or she is subjected to and the more complicated diving becomes. In very deep water divers have to breathe compressed air. However, if the body is subjected to too rapid a decrease in pressure, a life-threatening condition known as the bends results. In order to return to normal air pressure gradually, a diver must spend hours or even days in a decompression chamber. An atmospheric diving suit—which has a tough

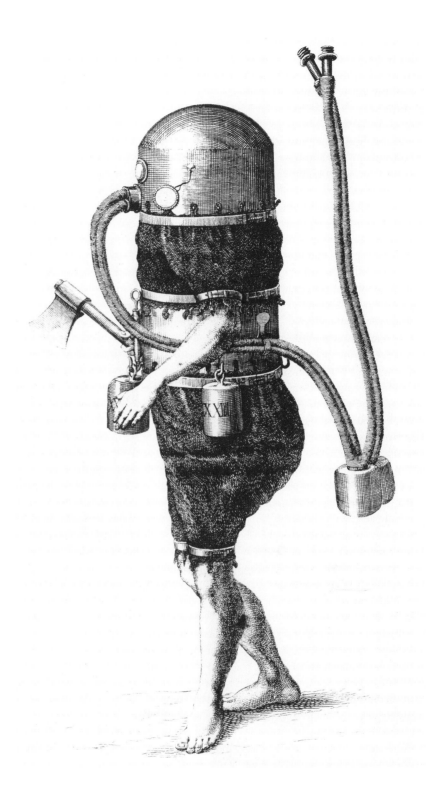

shell and moves with its own propellers and thrusters—can solve deep-water problems. Such suits maintain normal air pressure, even at depths of 1,000 feet (300 m).

Explorers in Space

Since astronauts first traveled to space in the 1960s, space suits have undergone great

Above **Early armored diving suits, such as this model from 1797, were imaginative but usually impractical.**

changes. The first space suits were based on flight suits worn by jet aircraft pilots. They were made of a rubber-coated neoprene covered with layers of aluminized Mylar (a polyester film). In the event of a cabin pressure failure, the suits could be pressurized to match the air pressure on earth; they also provided an oxygen supply.

Before space suits could be used outside the spacecraft, several improvements had to be made. The new suit was covered with netting and then with layers of nylon coated with Teflon (a synthetic resin); this combination protects the astronaut from micrometeoroids—tiny pieces of rock, dust, or space debris—which can inflict a great deal of damage on someone who gets in their way. An "umbilical cord" connects the space suit to the spacecraft and supplies oxygen and removes carbon dioxide. Cool air is pumped to the suit to make sure that during a spacewalk the astronaut does not become overheated or dehydrated.

Twenty-first-century space suits are made up of layers of synthetic fabrics, including neoprene, Gore-Tex, Dacron, Kevlar, and Mylar. Water-cooled garments prevent the wearer from overheating. Helmets are designed to reflect the sunlight while reducing its glare. Headsets with microphones and earphones linked to radio transmitters and receivers enable astronauts outside the spacecraft to talk to each other and to those who remain on board.

SEE ALSO

- Amundsen, Roald
- Astronauts • Polar Exploration
- Scott, Robert Falcon
- Underwater Exploration

Extravehicular Mobility Unit

*T*he Extravehicular Mobility Unit (EMU), the ultimate space suit, allows the astronaut to move freely around space. The EMU weighs 280 pounds (127 kg) on earth and has thirteen layers. Its parts are made in different sizes so that a complete suit can be put together to fit any astronaut. The EMU includes

- a garment to collect urine
- a garment to cool the astronaut
- a communications system
- upper and lower body sections with movable joints
- arms, gloves, and a helmet
- a visor designed to protect the wearer from bright sunlight
- a drink bag to help the astronaut avoid dehydration
- a support system that removes carbon dioxide and provides oxygen, power, cooling water, and radio equipment and can be operated by the astronaut
- an emergency oxygen supply

COLONIZATION AND CONQUEST

CONQUEST IS THE TAKING possession of a territory by force; colonization is the placement into a territory of settlers who are politically, economically, and militarily connected to their parent state. When joined, conquest and colonization involve the defeat of a people and the settling and ruling of its territory by its conquerors. Although seldom a concern for the conquerors, this sequence of events has usually had disastrous consequences for the conquered. Common in the ancient world, from the fifteenth century onward conquest and colonization came to be linked with exploration and practiced on a global scale.

THE PORTUGUESE IN AFRICA AND ASIA

The Portuguese and Spanish were the first to explore and develop the sea routes that eventually joined all parts of the globe. In 1385 the modern nation of Portugal emerged out of the recovery of territories that had been conquered by Muslim invaders in the seventh century. The ultimate success of this seven-hundred-year-long *Reconquista* (reconquest) gave the two Iberian nations immense self-confidence. Later Portuguese and Spanish expansion overseas was essentially a by-product of this triumph.

By the early fifteenth century Portugal had a stable economy and a monarchy that sought to expand its trade and roll back the tide of Islam. In 1415 Prince Henry the Navigator attacked and took Ceuta, a Muslim trading center on the Mediterranean shore of present-day Morocco. Unable to extend trade east into the Muslim-controlled Mediterranean, Henry began to send navigators on voyages of exploration west and south along the coast of Africa.

In the 1420s Madeira and the Azores became agricultural colonies, and by 1441 the Portuguese had reached Río de Oro (in present-day Western Sahara), where they joined in the slave trade that was eventually expanded along the coast of tropical Africa.

From 1480 the Portuguese began converting their trading sites into fortified bases. After Bartolomeu Dias rounded the Cape of Good Hope in 1488, the Portuguese expanded along the shores of the Indian Ocean to Malaysia, driving out many of their Muslim rivals in the process. Some major port cities became Portuguese trading centers.

In 1542 the Portuguese made contact with Japan and in 1555 established a base in Macao, China. The ruthlessness with which some Portuguese explorers carried out their search for wealth was an all-too-common phenomenon in a world where a resurgent and aggressive Ottoman Empire, having toppled Constantinople in 1453, was striking deep into the center of Europe.

SPAIN IN THE NEW WORLD

Like Portugal, Spain was formed after the expulsion of the Moors from the Iberian Peninsula and as an amalgamation of smaller kingdoms. In 1493, following Christopher Columbus's first voyage to the Americas, Pope Alexander VI, in response to a request from Queen Isabella of Spain, issued a bull (a formal, relatively brief papal letter) called *Inter Caetera*. Its main purpose was to prevent the territorial ambitions of Portugal and Spain from developing into protracted warfare in the New World and the Old and distracting both powers from the ongoing Muslim threat. With the 1494 Treaty of Tordesillas, Spain and Portugal divided the world at about 45 degrees west longitude, placing the western half under Spanish control and the eastern under Portuguese.

Columbus's four voyages led to the rapid colonization of the larger Caribbean islands. After local resistance was crushed, lands were distributed among the participants in the conquest, and most of the remaining indigenous population was enslaved. By 1511 Hispaniola, Puerto Rico, Jamaica, and Cuba were fully occupied and being commercially exploited, mainly through slave labor on agricultural estates and sugar plantations. In 1517 the first slaves from Africa were imported to replace the rapidly dying native population. Slavery persisted in the Americas for the next 350 years and more.

Between 1516 and 1518 the governor of Cuba sent expeditions to the Mexican mainland. Some returned with gold and stories of a wealthy civilization in the interior—that of the Aztecs. From 1519 to 1521, aided by the Aztecs' enemies and an outbreak of smallpox, a small force of Spanish adventurers destroyed the Aztec Empire. The surrounding countryside was seized and divided among the conquistadors. Over the next twenty-five years, Central America fell to Spain.

Similar developments occurred in South America. By 1535 a small army led by Francisco Pizarro had destroyed the empire of

Right **The conquest of the Americas was accompanied by the effort to convert the indigenous peoples to Christianity. The Church of Saint Augustine, built in 1613 at the Isleta Pueblo in New Mexico by the Franciscan friar Juan de Salas, was partially destroyed during the Pueblo Revolt of 1680 and rebuilt in 1716.**

Ancient Forms

One of the earliest documented forms of colonization linked to exploration was the establishment of Greek trading posts along the coasts of the Mediterranean and Black Seas during the eighth century BCE. As more Greek migrants arrived, these trading posts became commercial and agricultural colonies. In the western Mediterranean the Phoenicians built a similar system of colonies. The dual process of conquest and colonization is more clearly seen with the expansion of Rome into territories inhabited by the tribes of Gaul (58–51 BCE) and Britain (43 CE). Military garrisons were established at strategic places and were often joined by merchants and agricultural settlers. These settlers brought the Roman way of life to the local population, and the meeting of cultures often led to intermarriage.

the Incas. By 1536 what is now Peru was in Spanish hands, and expeditions were moving into Chile and across the Andes.

THE ENGLISH IN NORTH AMERICA

At first, the English, instead of seeking to establish their own American colonies, were content to rob Spanish ships as they returned from the Caribbean. In 1497 the Italian explorer John Cabot announced that the waters off Newfoundland in North America contained huge stocks of fish. Before long the English, as well as the French, the Basques, and the Portuguese, were there in force.

The first successful English colony was Jamestown (founded in 1607). The London Company of Virginia, a group of wealthy individuals, had obtained a charter from King James VI to establish a colony in Virginia (a territory that was several times the size of the modern state of Virginia).

Above **The landing of the Pilgrims at Plymouth, Massachusetts, on December 21, 1620, is an event with great symbolic importance in American history.**

To the north the Pilgrim Fathers arrived at Plymouth in 1620. In 1629, by which time the closely related Puritans had begun arriving, the colonists received a royal charter from King Charles I. The subsequent influx of settlers was rapid, and as the colony spread into the native people's land, conflicts arose. English reaction to the indigenous presence differed from that of the Portuguese and Spanish. Land was taken by force of arms, and the former residents driven into the interior. There was little attempt at accommodation in Massachusetts Bay colony, although relations were far more amicable in the breakaway colony of Rhode Island.

THE FRENCH IN NORTH AMERICA

By the 1580s the French controlled a small fur trade on the Atlantic coast of North America. In order to pursue trading more efficiently, posts had to be established. Because good relations with the American Indian peoples were necessary to pursue a fur trade and live in peace, King Henry IV of France made a treaty (1602–1603) with the Montagnais near present-day Tadoussac. This treaty gave the French permission to settle in the Saint Lawrence valley, providing they helped their new allies against their Iroquois enemies. Thus began a policy of cooperation between the French and the native peoples almost unique in the history of exploration and colonization in the New World. Efforts were made by the crown to contain French settlement along the Saint Lawrence River.

CAUSES AND RESULTS

The upsurge in exploration that began in the fifteenth century and led to widespread colonization and conquest is attributable to several factors: the search for wealth, the need to secure trade routes free from Ottoman control or threat, the desire of Christians to spread their faith, and the consequences of the wars and tensions that western Europe was experiencing both within and without its borders. In addition, for religious nonconformists especially, the opening of the New World offered a way out of difficult or even impossible situations at home.

The remarkable success of European colonization and conquest may or may not have been a foregone conclusion. Military superiority, especially in arms and tactics, and efficient systems of administration and government were major European pluses, as were Europe's superior transportation technologies, both on land and sea, and its advanced methods of food production, preservation, and storage, crop rotation, and livestock development. Furthermore, though unfamiliar diseases troubled Europeans, natural immunities, better nutrition, superior medicine, or some combination thereof

Christianizing Canada

The initial efforts of Franciscan Recollect friars between 1615 and 1628 to convert the native peoples in the French Canadian colonies largely failed. The Jesuits, who arrived in 1632, had more success. French colonization methods overall were much more benign than those of the Portuguese and Spanish. To encourage conversion and to create a people adapted to living in Canada, the Jesuit superiors and the first governor of Quebec, Samuel de Champlain, tried in 1635 to promote intermarriage between the French and, especially, the populous Huron. Although the intermarriage program proposed by the French was rejected by the Indians, intermarriage eventually became widespread—especially in the interior, where it helped promote good will in exploration, trade, and alliances.

Below **This engraving shows a French expedition landing at Anastasia Island, near Saint Augustine, Florida, in 1562. Although the French made friendly contact with local Timucuan natives, later French settlers were killed by rival Spanish forces.**

The British in Australia

*A*ustralia, claimed for Britain by James Cook in 1770, seemed to offer a solution to the problem of Britain's overcrowded prisons. Convicts were shipped to Australia and, after their sentence expired, were expected to become self-sufficient farmers on plots of land measuring between thirty and fifty acres. By 1867, when the last convicts were landed, Australia had received some 160,000. By the early 1800s free settlers were encouraged to emigrate to Australia, but their arrival was slow and uncertain. As the aboriginal people were nomadic hunters and gatherers, they were not regarded as owners of their land; hence, no treaties or land purchases were necessary to dispossess them. This land-acquisition policy was similar to that followed in the Americas. Aboriginals were eliminated whenever they tried to tried to defend their land or person. As in America, there were disastrous epidemics of smallpox and other diseases.

Above Unlike other districts in Australia, which colonized with convicts, Port Adelaide was settled by free settlers, such as the genteel people pictured here. Founded in 1837, by the mid-1840s Adelaide had a population of around 14,000.

worked to their advantage. Explorers and colonizers, in common with those they found or supplanted, suffered from the ravages of unfamiliar diseases, but the consequences were far less dire for the Europeans than for the native populations of the New World, Australia, and the islands of the Pacific.

SEE ALSO

• Cortés, Hernán • France • Great Britain • Missions
• Native Peoples • Portugal • Spain • Trade

COLUMBIAN EXCHANGE

THE PHRASE *COLUMBIAN EXCHANGE* was coined by the American historian Alfred Crosby, who used it as the title of his 1972 book. Crosby examined the results of the discovery and settlement of the Americas by Christopher Columbus and the Europeans who followed him. *Columbian exchange* describes the movement of people, plants, animals, diseases, technology, and ideas between the Old World of Europe, Asia, and Africa and the New World of the Americas.

For thousands of years, there was almost no contact between the peoples of Europe, Asia, and Africa (the Old World) and those of the territories discovered by Spanish explorers in the Western Hemisphere (the New World). In both regions human societies developed independently, each unaware of the other's existence, culture, language, modes of thought, and way of life. In 1492, when he sailed west from Spain and crossed the Atlantic to reach the Americas, Christopher Columbus, in Crosby's words, "brought the two halves of this planet together."

DISEASES

For many of the indigenous peoples of the Americas, the arrival of Columbus had disastrous consequences. Besides the threat represented by the Europeans' vastly superior military technology, American Indians suffered greatly from their lack of resistance to diseases such as smallpox, influenza, and measles. Such diseases, although commonplace in the Old World, were unfamiliar to inhabitants of the New World, and a sizable portion of the Indian population may have succumbed to them. (Europeans also suffered

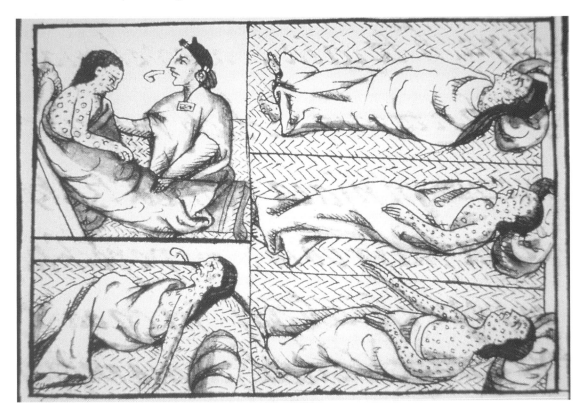

Left **This drawing of Native Americans dying of smallpox comes from an Aztec history of the Spanish conquest of Mexico. The text it illustrates reads, "We were covered with agonizing sores from head to foot. The illness was so dreadful that no one could walk or move."**

What Was Exchanged

From the Old World:	From the New World:
barley	avocados
cattle	chili peppers and
chickens	other peppers
Christianity	chocolate
coffee	grey squirrels
diseases, such as smallpox	insects, including colorado
and influenza	beetles
European languages	maize
gunpowder	manioc
horses	peanuts
insects, including cockroaches	pineapples
iron and steel	potatoes
oats	rubber
onions	squashes
pigs	sweet potatoes
rats	tobacco
rice	tomatoes
sheep	turkeys
tea	
wheat	
wheeled transport	

LABOR

For the conquering Europeans, the death of large numbers of Indians caused a labor shortage. The shortage was one of several factors that prompted an increase in transportation of enslaved Africans to the Americas, where they were put to work on sugar and cotton plantations and in gold and silver mines. From 1505 to 1852, between eight and eleven million Africans were shipped across the Atlantic, the vast majority of them to South America.

FOOD

Around the world the Columbian exchange led to increased food production, thanks mainly to the spread of useful crops, such as manioc (or cassava), a plant found by Columbus in South America. Manioc is high yielding, resists drought and pests, and can grow in the poorest soil. It has become the staple food crop grown in the world's tropical regions. Wheat, a crop that passed from the Old World to the New, now provides the world's people with 20 percent of their calorie intake. In 2000 wheat covered 96,000 square miles (250,000 km^2) of the United States.

One consequence of increased food production has been a vast increase in the world's population. Since 1492, when Columbus made his famous voyage across the Atlantic Ocean, the world's population has grown by a factor of ten.

from their encounters with unfamiliar diseases but to a lesser extent). In 1699 a missionary wrote, "The Indians die so easily that the bare look and smell of a Spaniard causes them to give up the ghost."

OCTOBER 12, 1492 Christopher Columbus reaches the islands of the Caribbean.	**1519–1520** Hernán Cortés conquers the Aztec Empire of Mexico, helped by a smallpox epidemic, which also sweeps through the Caribbean and Central America.	**c. 1525** The Portuguese introduce South American chili peppers to India.	**c. 1550** Chili peppers are first used in China.	**1602** Bartholomew Gosnold plants wheat and oats at Buzzards Bay, in Massachusetts.
1493 Columbus introduces horses, cattle, sheep, pigs, chickens, sugarcane, and wheat to the West Indies.	**1520** Tomatoes are brought to Spain from Mexico.	**1539** Hernando de Soto lands in Florida with 237 horses; some escape and breed in the wild.	**1562–1563** Smallpox sweeps through Brazil. **1563** John Hawkins brings tobacco and sweet potatoes to England.	**1607** The English build their first permanent settlement in North America at Jamestown, in Virginia.

Yet as humans and their domestic animals and food plants have spread, countless species of wild animals, birds, insects, and plants have become extinct. For better or worse, this aspect of the Columbian exchange continues to this day. The Great Plains, for example, whose wheat now feeds the world, were once home to wild grasses that were grazed by 60 million buffalo. In 2001 just 300,000 buffalo were left, and many of the grasses had gone forever.

Above **This 1787 picture shows a settler's farm in North America. When they crossed the Atlantic from the Old World to the New, European settlers brought with them a complete way of life.**

1629
The Portuguese introduce manioc, sweet potatoes, maize, and peanuts to West Africa.

1745
Plains Indians begin using horses to hunt buffalo.

SEE ALSO

• Colonization and Conquest
• Columbus, Christopher • Cortés, Hernán

COLUMBUS, CHRISTOPHER

Below **Columbus once said, "If one sails the seas, one will always find land." His confidence was borne out; his voyages are among the most important in the history of exploration.**

CHRISTOPHER COLUMBUS (Cristoforo Colombo, in Italian) was born in 1451 and died in 1506. In 1492 he set sail across the Atlantic Ocean, bound for China. Instead he found a previously unknown landmass, which came to be called the Americas. Although the Vikings had landed in Newfoundland five centuries earlier, it was Columbus, returning to Europe with news of the American continent, who transformed the outlook of the world.

Christopher Columbus was born into a family of weavers in the prosperous city of Genoa, Italy. A poorly educated boy, he became a sailor when he was fourteen. In about 1476 he was shipwrecked off the coast of Portugal and decided to settle there. In the following years, Columbus is believed to have sailed as far as northern England, the Cape Verde Islands (in the Atlantic Ocean), and Sierra Leone (on the western coast of Africa). He also learned how to read and write and make a map. About 1479 he married the daughter of a Portuguese nobleman.

ROUTES TO RICHES

In the fifteenth century India, Japan, Indonesia, and Southeast Asia were known to Europeans as the Indies. These distant lands were a treasure trove of spices, silk, gemstones, and other exotic goods. Overland voyages to China and the Indies were long and treacherous, and the ancient routes were dominated by Muslims. A direct and naviga-

1451
Columbus is born in Genoa, Italy.

1476
Moves to Lisbon, Portugal.

1479
Marries Felipa Perestrello e Moniz.

1477–1482
Sails to Iceland, the Cape Verde Islands, and Sierra Leone.

1484
King John II of Portugal refuses to back Columbus's proposed voyage across the Atlantic to the Indies.

1485
Felipa dies; Columbus moves to Spain.

APRIL 1492
King Ferdinand and Queen Isabella of Spain agree to support a voyage across the Atlantic.

AUGUST 3, 1492
Columbus departs from Palos, Spain, on first voyage.

OCTOBER 12, 1492
Land in the Americas.

OCTOBER 28, 1492
Reaches northeastern coast of Cuba.

DECEMBER 5, 1492
Arrives at Hispaniola.

MARCH 15, 1493
Returns to Spain.

SEPTEMBER 25, 1493
Departs from Cádiz on second voyage.

NOVEMBER 1493
Reaches Hispaniola.

Left **An artist's rendering of Columbus's landing in the New World. Believing he has reached Asia, Columbus plants the royal banner of Ferdinand and Isabella.**

ble water passage to the East would enable Europeans to share in the riches of the Indies.

Despite evidence to the contrary, the belief that the earth was flat—and that if sailors traveled far enough, they would fall off the edge of the world—was relatively widespread. Columbus's studies in the fields of geography and astronomy led him to conclude the earth was spherical. He suspected that the Asian continent stretched much farther to the east than most people thought. He also believed that if he traveled west across the Atlantic, he would reach the Indies.

In 1484 Columbus approached King John II of Portugal and asked him to finance an expedition to Japan. His ambitious plan failed

The Quadrant

To plot his route across the open ocean, Columbus used a compass and sometimes a quadrant. A quadrant is an instrument made from a quarter of a circle of metal. A small weight called a plumb is hung from the square corner of the quadrant on a piece of string. The plumb crosses the opposite edge of the arc, which is marked off with a scale that measures degrees. The navigator aims the quadrant at the North Star (or, by day, the sun) and is able to read the angle of the star above the horizon—that is, the star's altitude. This information can then be used to calculate the line of latitude the ship is following.

to gain the support of the king, and in 1485 Columbus headed to the court of Ferdinand and Isabella of Spain.

1495
Attempts conquest of Hispaniola.

MARCH 1496
Returns to Spain.

MAY 30, 1498
Departs from Sanlúcar, Spain, on third voyage

JULY 31, 1498
Arrives at Trinidad.

AUGUST 1498
Lands on South American continent; returns to Hispaniola.

OCTOBER 1500
Is arrested by Bobadilla and returns to Spain in chains.

MAY 9, 1502
Departs from Cádiz on final voyage.

JULY–SEPTEMBER 1502
Arrives in Hispaniola; explores Costa Rica, Nicaragua, Panama, Cuba, and Honduras.

NOVEMBER 7, 1503
Returns to Spain.

MAY 20, 1506
Dies at Valladolid, Spain.

SAILING THE SEA OF DARKNESS

In 1492 Ferdinand and Isabella finally agreed to finance Columbus's expedition across the Atlantic. Columbus would be granted 10 percent of the goods he brought home and would be made governor of any new lands he discovered. On August 3, 1492, a crew of between ninety and a hundred men boarded three ships, the *Pinta*, the *Niña*, and the *Santa María*, at Palos on the Atlantic coast of Spain. The flotilla set sail at dawn across an ocean known to sailors as the sea of darkness. Some of the crew feared they would never see their families again.

THE NEW WORLD

Less than a week later Columbus stopped at the Canary Islands to repair and refit his ships. On September 6 he left San Sebastián de la Gomera on a westward course, and after thirty-three days at sea, his men sighted land. On October 12, Columbus landed on the first of a string of islands now known as the Bahamas. Believing he had reached Asia, Columbus went ashore and planted the banner of Ferdinand and Isabella. He named the island San Salvador (Holy Savior) and pressed onward in search of Japan and the Indies. Soon after, he reached present-day Cuba. Convinced he had landed on the coast of China, he sent men to look for the Chinese emperor. On December 5 Columbus saw an island he thought so beautiful that he named it Hispaniola, after Spain. (The island is now divided between Haiti and the Dominican Republic.)

THE LAND OF PLENTY

On Hispaniola, Columbus encountered native inhabitants called the Taino (also known as the Island Arawak). Realizing that he was not in China but thinking that he had landed at least somewhere in the Indies, he called the natives Indios (Indians). Impressed by their gentle, friendly manner, he described their way of life in his journal. They ate a vegetable called *batata* (sweet potato). They slept in *hamacas*, which the Europeans would copy and call hammocks, and smoked dried leaves that they called *tabaca*. Columbus also noted the lavish gold jewelry that the Indians wore.

Right **A model of the *Santa María*, Columbus's flagship.**

Right **This 1494 pamphlet describes the construction of La Navidad fort on Hispaniola. At first, the settlers believed they had landed in paradise, but they were soon beset by disease and by conflicts with the native people.**

HOMEWARD BOUND

Columbus's flagship, the *Santa María*, sank off the coast of Hispaniola on December 24, 1492. The wreckage of the ship may have been used to build a fort at Hispaniola, which Columbus named La Navidad (Christmas). On January 16, 1493, Columbus set sail on the *Niña* from La Navidad for Spain. He left behind about forty of his crew and took with him six Indians and examples of gold and jewelry to impress Ferdinand and Isabella. He arrived home on March 15. The king and queen were delighted with his discoveries and were happy to finance a second expedition to the Indies. Columbus's mission was to colonize Hispaniola, to explore Cuba in order to determine whether it was an island or part of the Asian mainland, and to bring back more riches.

THE SECOND VOYAGE

On October 13 Columbus set sail from Hierro on the Canary Islands with seventeen ships carrying more than a thousand men, food, wine, livestock, plants, and tools. It was the largest expedition to colonize a foreign land ever launched. On November 3, after twenty-one days at sea, Columbus sighted the island of Dominica, part of the West Indies, where he encountered the warlike Caribs, an Indian people who ate human flesh. (The Taino called them "cannibals.") The fleet sailed on to the Leeward Islands, the Virgin Islands, and Puerto Rico before arriving at Hispaniola on November 22. When Columbus returned to La Navidad, he found the fort had been burned down and the men he had left behind had been murdered by the Indians.

Tav. VI. pag 282.

The Taino

A local chief told Columbus what had happened at La Navidad. The chief claimed that the Spaniards had provoked the Indians by kidnapping local women. This unfortunate situation involving the local people set the pattern for future colonization of the West Indies. The unaggressive Taino Indians were used as slaves, and their pre-Columbian culture disappeared with their conversion to Christianity. Many Taino died through overwork and lack of immunity to European diseases. Fifty years after the first Spaniards arrived at Hispaniola, only 500 Taino Indians remained alive of an original population of around 300,000.

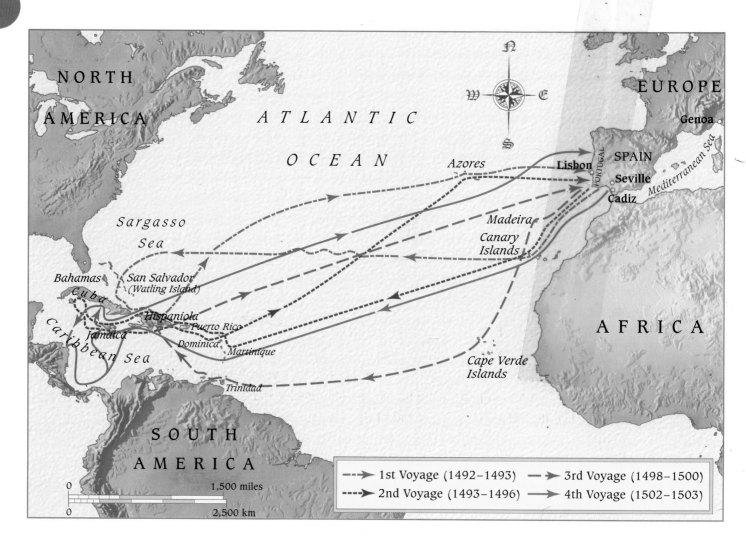

Above **This map shows the four epic journeys that Columbus made across the so-called sea of darkness.**

Columbus continued eastward along the northern coast of Hispaniola and founded a new settlement, which he named La Isabella after the Spanish queen. He still had not found Japan and China nor had he discovered the gold he had promised Isabella and Ferdinand. On April 24, 1494, Columbus set off to find China. He reached Cuba on May 3. Following a six-week survey of Cuba's southern coast, Columbus wrongly concluded that it was an Asian peninsula. After becoming seriously ill, however, he gave up any further exploration. He left his brother Bartolomeo in charge at Hispaniola and in March 1496 returned to Spain.

A GREAT CONTINENT

Isabella and Ferdinand's faith in Columbus had begun to wane, and so for his third voyage they provided only six ships.

Columbus departed on May 30, 1498. Half the fleet sailed to Hispaniola laden with supplies. Columbus explored farther south, but the expedition was beset with problems. The ships were becalmed in the doldrums, an area where there is a lack of wind, and they were down to their last barrel of water when they finally sighted land. On July 31, 1498, Columbus arrived at an island he called La Trinidad (Holy Trinity). Days later, on August 5, he landed at the Gulf of Paria, in present-day Venezuela, and thus became the first European to set foot on the South American mainland. In his journal Columbus said he had found "a very great continent ... where Christianity will have so much enjoyment."

When Columbus returned to Hispaniola, he was a sick man, and the colonists had revolted. Isabella and Ferdinand heard about the problems at Hispaniola and sent the nobleman Francisco de Bobadilla to restore order. Columbus and his brothers Bartolomeo and Diego were detained and sent home to Spain in chains. Upon his return Columbus was released, but he was not allowed to govern in the Indies again.

THE FINAL VOYAGE

Columbus felt bitter about his treatment, yet he was determined to regain his fortune and his good name. He applied to Isabella and Ferdinand to finance another expedition. On May 9, 1502, Columbus led a fleet of 4 ships and 141 men on his last voyage to the Americas. Still convinced that he had found a route to Asia, he was determined to find a strait linking the Indies with the Indian Ocean. He sailed along the southern edge of the Gulf of Mexico and visited Honduras, Nicaragua, Costa Rica, and Panama, believing that he was exploring the Malay Peninsula in Southeast Asia. At Panama, Indians attacked him, and one of his ships was sunk in a storm

Columbus describes La Isabella, an island in the Bahamas:

My eyes are never tired with viewing such delightful verdure, and of a species so new and dissimilar to that of our country, and I have no doubt there are trees and herbs here which would be of great value in Spain, as dyeing materials, medicine, spicery, etc.

Christopher Columbus, *Journal of the First Journey*

off the coast. After losing another ship, Columbus and his men were marooned on the island of Jamaica for a year. A rescue ship did not arrive until June 29, 1503.

Columbus arrived back in Spain in November 1503. Too ill to take to the high seas again, he settled in Seville. He died on May 20, 1506, in Valladolid and was buried in a monastery near Seville.

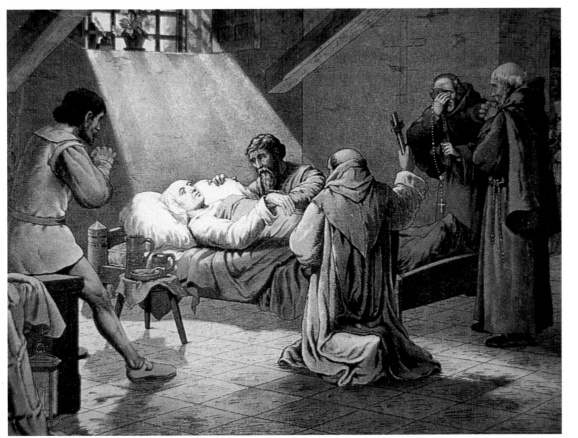

Left **Surrounded by his sons, Columbus died in poverty at Valladolid, in northern Spain, and was buried in a monastery in Seville, in southern Spain.**

SEE ALSO
- Ferdinand and Isabella
- Spain

COMMUNICATION DEVICES

Below **Polar explorer Ollie Shepherd communicates by radio during his 1988 expedition to the North Pole.**

FOR QUICK AND EFFICIENT COMMUNICATION, the people involved must be able to see or hear each other. Explorers frequently find themselves isolated and in danger, and a range of communication methods and devices have been invented to enable an urgent message to be transmitted over long distances.

In the twenty-first century explorers have at their disposal a range of technologically advanced methods of communication. Wherever they are in the world, they can stay in touch with a support team and, if necessary, ask for help. For the first explorers, however, methods of long-distance communication were were either unavailable or very basic, and a message could take weeks, months, or even years to reach its destination.

Many explorers who might have been saved had communication devices been available died because they had no way of asking for help. For example, Robert Falcon Scott and his team of Antarctic explorers, who froze to death in 1912, might have survived if they had they been able to communicate with the rest of their expedition.

EARLY COMMUNICATION

Unable to send long-distance messages, ancient explorers left signs for those that followed later. A pile of stones or a mark carved into a tree, for example, showed that explorers had reached a certain place and indicated the direction in which they were traveling.

---

c. 1200
Genghis Khan uses homing pigeons to send messages.

1405
Chinese sailors communicate using bells and flags.

1794
Claude Chappe invents semaphore in France.

1831
Joseph Henry invents the electric telegraph.

c. 1838
Samuel Morse invents Morse code.

1843
The world's first public telegraph line opens in Britain.

1851
The first underwater telegraph cable is laid across the English Channel.

1858
Queen Victoria sends the first transatlantic telegram to the United States.

1876
Alexander Graham Bell invents the telephone.

1895
Gugliemo Marconi invents wireless telegraphy.

1912
The first telemetry system is installed in Chicago.

As people began to travel greater distances, better and faster forms of communication developed. One method was the relay system, whereby a messenger would carry information to a second messenger, who would carry the information to a third messenger, and so on. In this way urgent news could be sent across great distances. The Mongolian warrior Genghis Khan (c. 1160–1227) used homing pigeons to send important messages at great speed.

By the fifteenth century sailors were using increasingly inventive forms of communication. The great Chinese navigator Cheng Ho (c. 1371–1435) commanded a huge fleet. His ships used banners, bells, flags, lanterns, and gongs to send messages back and forth.

COMMUNICATING WITHOUT SPEECH

The idea of sending messages over distance from hill to hill dates back centuries. A chain of signal fires was one effective way of sending a warning or other simple message to a distant place.

In 1794 Claude Chappe invented semaphore, a system that allowed more-complicated messages to be sent from one place to another. High towers were built a few miles apart from each other in a long line. The towers were fitted with movable arms that could be set in different positions, each position representing a letter or number. With the aid of a telescope, the lookout on the next tower would record the

Morse Code

Samuel Morse designed Morse code in about 1838. He assigned each letter of the alphabet a combination of dots and dashes, representing short and long electrical pulses, respectively. The most commonly used letters were given the shortest signals.

A	.–	J	.– – –	S	...
B	–...	K	–.–	T	–
C	–.–.	L	.–..	U	..–
D	–..	M	– –	V	...–
E	.	N	–.	W	.– –
F	..–.	O	– – –	X	–..–
G	– –.	P	.– –.	Y	–.– –
H	....	Q	– –.–	Z	– –..
I	..	R	.–.		

message and pass it on. Semaphore enabled the relatively quick transmission of more-detailed messages.

Below **Samuel Morse (1791–1872) demonstrates how to operate his Morse key transmitter.**

1940
The German post office starts the first video telephone service.

1946
The first mobile telephone system is introduced in the United States.

JULY 10, 1962
Telstar 1, the first active satellite, is launched.

1988
The first transatlantic fiber-optic link comes into use.

The telegraph proved a much more useful communication device to explorers. Early in the nineteenth century Joseph Henry (1797–1878) and Samuel F. B. Morse (1791–1872) developed an electric telegraph system that allowed electrical pulses to be transmitted along wires. Morse code, invented around 1838, was a means of coding words into strings of electrical pulses; a message sent by this method was called a telegram. As soon as an explorer reached a telegraph office, he or she could send a telegram home. In 1953, the London *Times* printed the exclusive story of Edmund Hillary's ascent of Mount Everest. Their journalist had raced down the mountain and sent a telegram from a Nepal telegraph office.

Distress Signals

The most important method of communication on sea voyages is the distress signal. Throughout history explorers and sailors on board a ship in distress have used many methods to attract the attention of rescuers. Flares, for example, can be heard and seen for miles around and continue to be used in the twenty-first century.

An explorer marooned on an island or stranded in a coastal area far from civilization has few options. In the fortunate event of a ship passing close by, its attention might be attracted by any available means, such as gunshots, flares, mirrors, or fires. A written message put inside a bottle and thrown into the sea is a last resort and rarely succeeds.

SOS is a distress signal that has been recognized throughout the world since around 1900. The letters are said to stand for "save our souls," and when converted into Morse code (. . . _ _ _ . . .), they can be transmitted in a number of different ways. By day flashes of sunlight can be directed toward another ship or to people on shore by means of a heliograph—a device consisting of movable mirrors. By night a flashing light fulfills the same function. With the invention of the radio came the international radio distress call Mayday. This word derives from the French phrase *m'aider*, meaning "help me."

Wireless Communication

Less than fifty years after the invention of the electric telegraph, Alexander Graham Bell (1847–1922) invented the telephone, an instrument that made it possible for two people to speak to each other over a great distance. Telephones, however, require a wire connection—seldom, if ever, available in the remote regions targeted by explorers.

Wireless radio was a giant leap forward in communication. Radio transmission is the sending and receiving of electromagnetic radiation, especially electromagnetic waves carrying audio messages, through the earth's atmosphere. In 1895 Guglielmo Marconi sent the first radio signals over long distances. At first, radio was called wireless telegraphy, as the radio waves carried only coded electrical pulses. By 1906 Lee de Forest had discovered way of magnifying weak signals so that voices could be clearly transmitted. Explorers wishing to communicate no longer had to rely on finding a telegraph station or a telephone. All they required was a radio set.

On August 16, 1858, Queen Victoria sent the first transatlantic telegram from London to President James Buchanan in Washington, DC. The message, an excerpt of which follows, took over sixteen hours to transmit.

The queen desires to congratulate the president upon the successful completion of this great international work, in which the queen has taken the deepest interest. The queen is convinced that the president will join with her in fervently hoping that the electric cable which now connects Great Britain with the United States will prove an additional link between the nations whose friendship is founded upon their common interest and reciprocal esteem. The queen has much pleasure in thus communicating with the president.

Left **Guglielmo Marconi, photographed in England in 1896 with his new invention, the "black box" wireless telegraphy device.**

Satellite and Telephone Communication

In 1962 *Telstar 1* became the first satellite to transmit a telephone conversation across the Atlantic. A spoken message was sent up to the satellite from the earth's surface as a radio signal and then transmitted back down to a different location. *Telstar* was also able to receive and transmit the sound and pictures of television programs.

These early telephone conversations transmitted via satellites were subject to short delays as the signal traveled to and from the satellite. In the late twentieth century newly developed fiber-optic cables laid in many parts of the world were able to carry thousands of telephone calls at a time without any delays. By the 1990s several innovations had helped to revolutionize communication, with great benefits for explorers and people in remote places. Cellular phones gave people freedom to speak from many more locations. Videophones allowed callers to see the person to whom they were speaking.

Right **On July 20, 1969, radio waves were used to transmit live coverage of the first moon landing. In Montreal, Canada, thousands gathered to watch the moon walk on a large screen.**

TELEMETRY

Telemetry is a communication process that allows measurements to be automatically taken from very remote places—even from space—and transmitted elsewhere for recording and analysis. Information is usually transmitted by radio signal.

Telemetry has many uses. It allows explorers to monitor weather conditions around the world. It also enables spaceflights to be controlled from earth. Scientists can communicate with unmanned spacecraft and also monitor and record conditions on manned spaceflights; as a result, astronauts have more time to carry out hands-on procedures.

UNDERWATER COMMUNICATION DEVICES

The seabed is one of the least explored and most dangerous places on earth. Explorers who venture beneath the surface of the sea have to cope with extreme conditions, such as low visibility, freezing water, and high water pressure. It is essential that they remain in contact with their support vessel at all times. Radio waves do not travel well under water, so other communication methods must be used.

Divers communicate with each other using hand signals or wipe boards on which messages can be written. In case of emergency, a diver-recall signal—a kind of giant firework—is thrown into the sea. This signal tells divers to return to the surface at once.

Deep sea divers are attached to their support vessel with an umbilical cord, providing them with air to breathe, heated water to keep them warm, and a communication link. A microphone built into the breathing apparatus allows the diver to talk to people above water. Submarines on exploration voyages use a similar cord to stay in touch with the support boat above.

Arthur C. Clarke B. 1917

Arthur C. Clarke was born in Minehead, England. He is one of the world's best-known science fiction authors, and many of his writings contain ideas about future technology. In an article entitled "Extra-Terrestrial Relays—Can Rocket Stations Give Worldwide Radio Coverage?" Clarke wrote that a space station in orbit above the earth "could be provided with receiving and transmitting equipment . . . to relay transmissions between any two points on the hemisphere beneath." These thoughts about the possibilities of satellite communication were published in 1945, more than ten years before satellites were actually launched into space.

COOK, JAMES

JAMES COOK (1728–1779) rose through the ranks of the British Royal Navy until he was in command of his own ships. During a ten-year period in the mid-1700s, Cook made three momentous voyages to the South Pacific. His discoveries of new lands, peoples, plants, and animals redrew the map of the world.

Below **Captain James Cook, explorer of the South Pacific.**

FROM ERRAND BOY TO SAILOR

James Cook was born on October 27, 1728, in Marton, a village in northeastern England. At the age of sixteen, he was sent by his father to work for a grocer in a nearby fishing village on the North Sea coast, where his meetings with sailors convinced him that he wanted to go to sea. At seventeen he moved to the port of Whitby and was apprenticed to John Walker, who owned colliers (ships that transported coal). He taught himself mathematics and astronomy and quickly mastered the craft of navigation.

MASTER IN THE ROYAL NAVY

In 1755 Cook joined the Royal Navy as an able-bodied seaman, the lowest level. However, his skills as a navigator soon earned him promotion to the rank of master (navigating officer). At this time Britain was fighting the Seven Years' War (1756–1763) with France over possession of Canada. In 1759 Cook surveyed the Saint Lawrence River, and his maps helped the British take Quebec the following year. Cook's coastal surveys of Newfoundland

---

1728
Cook is born at Marton, in northeastern England.

1755
Joins the Royal Navy.

1759
Surveys the Saint Lawrence River in Canada.

1763–1767
Surveys Newfoundland and nearby islands.

1768–1771
First voyage to the South Pacific in search of the "great southern continent"; Cook charts the coasts of New Zealand and eastern Australia.

1772–1775
Second voyage to the South Pacific in search of the southern continent; Cook makes the first known crossing of the Antarctic Circle; circumnavigates Antarctica.

1776–1780
Third voyage to the South Pacific in search of the Northwest Passage; Cook explores the west coast of North America as far north as Alaska.

1779
Is killed on Hawaii during his third voyage.

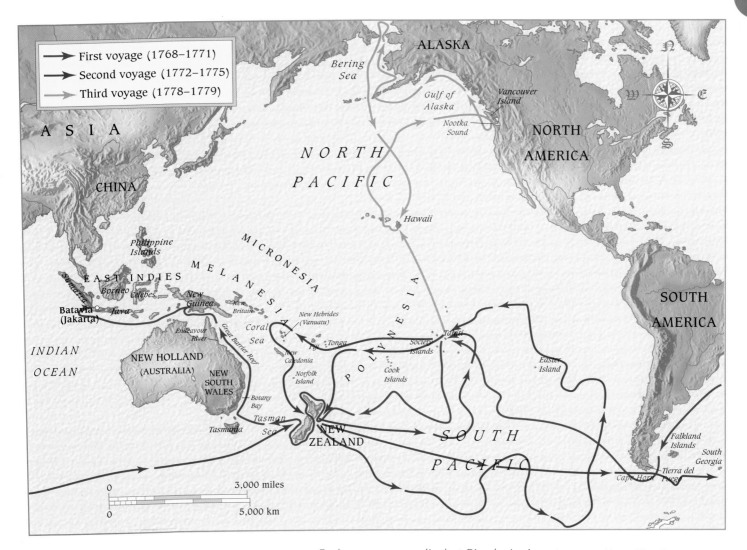

First voyage (1768–1771)
Second voyage (1772–1775)
Third voyage (1778–1779)

ALASKA

Bering Sea

Gulf of Alaska

Vancouver Island

Nootka Sound

NORTH AMERICA

A S I A

CHINA

N O R T H

P A C I F I C

Hawaii

Philippine Islands

M I C R O N E S I A

EAST INDIES

M E L A N E S I A

Borneo Celebes

Batavia (Jakarta) Java

New Guinea

New Britain

New Hebrides (Vanuatu)

Coral Sea

Great Barrier Reef

Endeavour River

INDIAN OCEAN

NEW HOLLAND (AUSTRALIA)

NEW SOUTH WALES

Botany Bay

Tasman Sea

Tasmania

NEW ZEALAND

Fiji Tonga

New Caledonia

Norfolk Island

P O L Y N E S I A

Cook Islands

Society Islands Tahiti

Easter Island

SOUTH AMERICA

S O U T H

P A C I F I C

Falkland Islands

South Georgia

Tierra del Fuego

Cape Horn

0   3,000 miles

0   5,000 km

Above **The three voyages of James Cook (1768–1779).**

between 1763 and 1767 were so accurate that they remained in use for the next two hundred years.

COOK'S FIRST PACIFIC VOYAGE

In 1768 the Royal Society of London and the Royal Navy appointed Cook leader of an expedition to the island of Tahiti in the South Pacific, from where the forthcoming transit of Venus would be observed. The expedition was to take measurements that would then be used to help navigators calculate a ship's longitude (its position to the east or west of a given meridian) more accurately.

On August 2, 1768, Lieutenant Cook sailed from Plymouth, England. His ship, the *Endeavour*, had a crew of about eighty sailors and a team of eleven scientists, including the botanist Joseph Banks (1744–1820). The *Endeavour* resupplied at Rio de Janiero, traveled around Cape Horn, and after thirty-three weeks at sea, reached Tahiti, where Cook observed the transit on June 3, 1769. His orders were then to search for the so-called *terra australis* (southern continent), a huge landmass in the Southern Hemisphere whose existence had never been proven.

The Health of Cook's Men

One of the hazards of long sea voyages was scurvy, a disease that weakened and killed sailors. It was brought on by a lack of vitamin C in their diet. Cook's men were issued a daily ration of fresh fruit and vegetables, especially orange and lemon juice, carrot marmalade, and sauerkraut (pickled cabbage), all of which are high in vitamin C. Cook's men stayed healthy, and not one died of scurvy on any of his three voyages.

The *Endeavour* sailed west to New Zealand, and over the next six months Cook made the first detailed survey of that country's coastline. Abel Tasman had been the first to locate New Zealand, in 1642, but Cook was the first to discover that it comprised two separate islands. At the end of March 1770, the *Endeavour* left New Zealand, and a storm blew the ship off course. On April 19, 1770, after nearly three weeks at sea, land was sighted. Cook had chanced upon the southeastern coast of Australia, then called New Holland—the name it was given by a Dutch explorer, Willem Jansz, the first European to land there (in 1605).

The *Endeavour* sailed along Australia's east coast and anchored in a bay on April 28. When the men went ashore, Joseph Banks found many new plants. His rich botanical discoveries gave the area its name: Botany Bay. Continuing his exploration of the Australian coastline, Cook sailed northward along the 1,250-mile (2,000 km) Great Barrier Reef. At one point the *Endeavour* was holed by the reef's sharp coral and narrowly escaped being wrecked. On August 21, 1770, Cook landed at Australia's most northerly point (the present-day Cape York Peninsula). He had become the first European to map Australia's east coast and claimed the region for Britain under the name New South Wales.

Cook returned home in July 1771. In the report of his voyage that he gave to the Royal Society and the Royal Navy, he described the geography of New Zealand and Australia and the people he had met (Polynesians in Tahiti, Maoris in New Zealand, and Australian aborigines). He brought back plants and animals never before seen in Europe, including Australian marsupials, such as the kangaroo.

Right **A cross section of the *Endeavour*, Captain Cook's ship on his first Pacific voyage (1768–1771).**

COOK'S SECOND PACIFIC VOYAGE

Although Cook had failed to find the southern continent, the Royal Society and the Royal Navy still believed it existed. A second expedition was organized, with Cook again chosen as leader. In July 1772 two ships left Plymouth: the *Resolution*, under Captain Cook's command, and the *Adventure*, under the command of Tobias Furneaux. Cook's plan was to continue sailing south until he reached land. If a continent did exist, he reasoned, he was bound to run across it.

The *Resolution* made the first known crossing of the Antarctic Circle, on January 17, 1773, but became separated from the *Adventure* among the icebergs. Cook decided it was too dangerous to stay in the area and crossed the South Pacific to New Zealand, where he rejoined the *Adventure*. In 1773 Cook toured the Pacific in the *Resolution* and

became the first European to visit a number of Pacific islands. Meanwhile, in October 1773 the *Adventure* sailed back to England.

The *Resolution* sailed south to complete Cook's exploration of the southern oceans and unknowingly circumnavigated Antarctica. Cook thus proved that there was no southern continent, only an icy wasteland. On his way home Cook rounded Cape Horn and discovered the South Sandwich Islands and South Georgia. He arrived back in Britain in July 1775.

Left **The Australian red honeysuckle tree was one of many plant species first brought to England from Australia on the *Endeavour*.**

Cook visited Easter Island in March 1774 and on March 17 wrote down his impressions of what he found:

No Nation will ever contend for the honor of the discovery of Easter Island as there is hardly an Island in this sea which affords less refreshments and conveniences for Shipping than it does; Nature has hardly provided it with any thing fit for man to eat or drink, and as the Natives are but few and may be supposed to plant no more than sufficient for themselves, they cannot have much to spare to new comers.

James Cook, *Journal*

COOK'S THIRD PACIFIC VOYAGE

The purpose of Cook's third voyage, like that of his first two, was to solve a geographical mystery. His orders were to find the western entrance to the Northwest Passage, a sea route around or through North America that Europeans hoped would provide them with a direct navigable passage to East Asia.

Cook sailed in the *Resolution* from Plymouth in July 1776. A second ship, the *Discovery*, was commanded by Charles Clerke. Cook's route took the ships around the Cape of Good Hope to New Zealand, Tahiti, and then north to a group of islands that he named the Sandwich Islands (the present-day Hawaiian Islands). After a period spent

Below **A depiction of Captain Cook meeting an untimely death on a Hawaiian beach in a skirmish with angry islanders.**

> ### Cook's Legacy
>
> James Cook's three voyages are remarkable for what they did not find as much as for what they did. Cook proved that no southern continent existed (apart, that is, from Antarctica). He also cast doubt on the existence of a northwest passage. With his accurate maps and records Cook did more than any other explorer to advance knowledge of the geography and people of the South Pacific islands. His exploration of New Zealand and Australia led to British colonization of those lands.

studying the islands and their people, Cook continued north along the west coast of North America to Prince William Sound and the Bering Sea, off the coast of Alaska.

In January 1779 the *Resolution* and the *Discovery* returned to the Sandwich Islands. The two ships anchored off the main island, Hawaii, and Cook and his men went ashore. The islanders treated them as if they were gods. After a few weeks they left but returned soon afterward when the *Resolution* needed repairs. Cook was not made welcome the second time, and on February 14, 1779, he was killed by islanders during a skirmish on the beach. Following the attack, Clerke took command of the expedition. He demanded the return of Cook's remains, which he then buried at sea. The *Resolution* and the *Discovery* returned to Britain in August 1780, having failed to find a northern sea route but carrying a profitable cargo of seal furs.

SEE ALSO

- Banks, Joseph
- Exploration and Geographical Societies
- Great Britain
- Northwest Passage

CORONADO, FRANCISCO VÁSQUEZ DE

THE SPANISH CONQUISTADOR and explorer Francisco Vásquez de Coronado (1510–1554) led the most significant early exploration of present-day Texas, Arizona, and New Mexico, a journey that laid the foundation for later Spanish claims to the American West.

EARLY LIFE

Francisco Coronado was born into an aristocratic family. As a young man at the Spanish court, he became friendly with Antonio de Mendoza (1490–1552), who in 1535 was named first viceroy of New Spain (present-day Mexico). When Mendoza set off for the Americas, he chose Coronado, then aged twenty-five, to be his assistant.

Within three years Coronado had made a significant impact; he suppressed a slave rebellion and pacified local Indians. He married Beatriz Estrada, daughter of the colonial treasurer, in 1538, the year Mendoza appointed him governor of New Galícia, a province on the west coast of New Spain.

IN SEARCH OF GOLD

In 1536 a group of Spaniards on a slave-taking mission in northern Mexico came across Álvar Núñez Cabeza de Vaca, a wild-looking man who had been given up for dead in Florida eight years earlier. He told of fabulous riches to be found in the Seven Golden Cities of Cibola. In 1539 Coronado sent an expedition north under Fray Marcos de Niza. When Fray Marcos returned, he verified Cabeza de Vaca's report.

His appetite whetted, Coronado assembled a huge expedition of over three hundred Spanish soldiers and eight hundred Native Americans, together with horses and herds of sheep, pigs, and cattle.

Right **A depiction of Coronado as he looked setting off on his journey in search of the fabled Seven Golden Cities.**

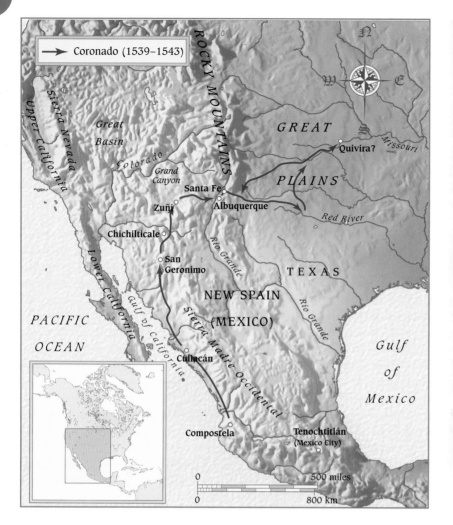

ROCKY MOUNTAINS
Sierra Nevada
Upper California
Great Basin
Colorado
Grand Canyon
GREAT PLAINS
Quivira?
Missouri
Santa Fe
Zuñi
Albuquerque
Chichilticale
Red River
Rio Grande
San Geronimo
TEXAS
PACIFIC OCEAN
Lower California
Gulf of California
NEW SPAIN (MEXICO)
Sierra Madre Occidental
Rio Grande
Gulf of Mexico
Culiacán
Compostela
Tenochtitlán (Mexico City)

0   500 miles
0   800 km

Above **The route taken by Coronado and his party through what is now the southern United States.**

The following is part of a statement that Spanish soldiers read to Native Americans—usually without translation—before taking their land:

We ask and require you that you . . . acknowledge the Church as the ruler and superior of the whole world, and the high priest called Pope, and in his name the king and queen.

If you do not do this . . . we shall powerfully enter into your country, and shall make war against you in all ways and manners that we can . . . we shall take you, and your wives, and your children, and shall make slaves of them . . . and we shall take away your goods, and shall do you all the mischief and damage that we can.

Juan Lopez de Palacios Rubios,
El Requirimento (1510)

The Seven Golden Cities of Cibola turned out to be pueblos (simple Native American villages) in present-day New Mexico. No gold or silver was found. Instead Coronado encountered the mud brick houses of a people who lived a simple life raising corn and beans. Fray Marcos admitted that he had merely seen the Seven Golden Cities from a distance. He was sent back to Mexico in disgrace.

EXPLORATION OF THE AMERICAN INTERIOR

Coronado refused to give up. A series of smaller groups broke off from the main expedition to explore vast areas of what is now the southwestern United States. Two ships under the command of Hernando de Alarcón discovered the mouth of the Colorado River and explored its lower reaches. García López

de Cárdenas and his party became the first Europeans to view the Grand Canyon (in present-day Arizona).

THE TURK

In 1541 a Pawnee Indian nicknamed the Turk told Coronado of the fabled wealth of the land of Quivira (present-day Kansas). Coronado left the main body of his men and journeyed farther north with thirty-six horsemen but found only a simple community of Wichita Indians. The Turk admitted that he had planned to lead Coronado's men onto the Texas plains and lose them and thus protect the Texan natives. Coronado executed him and began the long march back home.

RETURN TO MEXICO

When Coronado returned to Mexico empty-handed in 1542, Mendoza pronounced the

expedition a disastrous failure, and in 1544 an official inquiry found Coronado guilty of mistreatment of Native Americans under his authority. He was removed from office and took up a modest position in Mexico City, where he lived until his death in 1554.

It was not until decades later, when the chronicle of his expedition was published and the Spanish were gaining a firm foothold in southwestern North America, that the importance of Coronado's expeditions came to be recognized.

SEE ALSO
- Cabeza de Vaca, Álvar Núñez
- Narváez, Pánfilo de • Spain

Above **In search of the fabled seven cities, Coronado found only simple pueblos, such as the one pictured here at Acoma, New Mexico.**

1510
Coronado is born into a noble family in Salamanca, Spain.

1535
Travels to Mexico as assistant to Antonio de Mendoza, first viceroy of New Spain.

1537
Wins praise for putting down a slave rebellion.

1538
Marries the daughter of the colonial treasurer; is appointed governor of New Galícia.

1540
Is chosen by Mendoza to lead an expedition north; one of the party, García López de Cárdenas, becomes the first European to see the Grand Canyon.

1541
Coronado fails to find the fabled land of Quivira but explores the Great Plains as far north as present-day Kansas.

1542
Returns to New Spain.

1544
Is charged with corruption and negligence; takes up modest position in Mexico City.

1554
Dies in Mexico City.

CORTÉS, HERNÁN

HERNÁN CORTÉS (1485–1547) is one of the most important figures in the history of exploration and conquest. He discovered and destroyed the previously unknown Aztec Empire and in so doing added the colony of New Spain (present-day Mexico) to the Spanish Empire. His successes laid the foundation for further Spanish conquests in Central and South America. Though a great military strategist with a reputation for courage and single-mindedness, Cortés died poor, overlooked, and disillusioned.

IMPATIENT YOUTH

Hernán Cortés's parents were both from noble Spanish families that had little money. At the age of fourteen, Cortés was sent to study law in Salamanca. After two years he left the University of Salamanca and spent time in the ports of southern Spain. Having heard of Columbus's discoveries in the West Indies, he longed to go to sea. In 1504 Cortés sailed for the island of Hispaniola.

Right **Until the arrival of Cortés, Indians in the Americas had never seen horses, let alone mounted soldiers.**

1485
Cortés is born in Medellín, Spain.

1499
Is sent to the University of Salamanca.

1504
Sails for Hispaniola.

1511
Takes part in the conquest of Cuba.

1518
Is appointed captain-general by Velázquez for the expedition to the Yucatán.

1519
Wins over Tabasco and meets la Malinche; founds Veracruz; conquers Tenochtitlán.

1520
Marches against a rival Spanish force; returns to find Tenochtitlán in chaos and withdraws his forces during the *noche triste*.

1521
Reorganizes his forces and recaptures Tenochtitlán, an event that marks the downfall of the Aztec Empire.

1523
Is appointed governor of the colony of New Spain.

1524–1526
Spends two years in the jungles of Honduras.

1527
Is accused of killing Luis Ponce de Léon and is forced to retire.

1528
Sails to Spain to plead his case to the king.

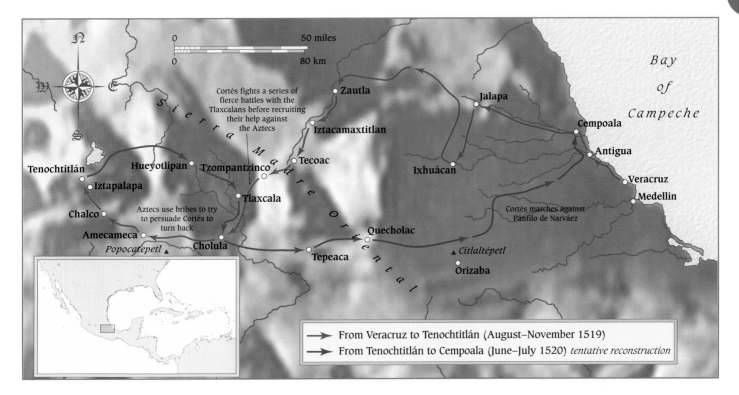

Map labels:

0 / 50 miles
0 / 80 km

Bay of Campeche

Zautla
Jalapa
Cempoala
Antigua
Cortés fights a series of fierce battles with the Tlaxcalans before recruiting their help against the Aztecs
Iztacamaxtitlan
Tecoac
Ixhuácan
Veracruz
Medellin
Tenochtitlán
Hueyotlipan
Tzompantzinco
Iztapalapa
Tlaxcala
Chalco
Aztecs use bribes to try to persuade Cortés to turn back
Quecholac
Cortés marches against Pánfilo de Narváez
Amecameca
Cholula
Popocatepetl
Tepeaca
Citlaltépetl
Orizaba

Sierra Madre Oriental

→ From Veracruz to Tenochtitlán (August–November 1519)
→ From Tenochtitlán to Cempoala (June–July 1520) *tentative reconstruction*

THE CONQUEST OF CUBA

Cortés spent six years in Hispaniola, during which time he impressed Diego Velázquez, a senior figure in the colonial administration. In 1511 Velázquez took Cortés with him on his journey to conquer Cuba. Velázquez was appointed governor of Cuba and included Cortés among his staff. Cortés became known for his excellent leadership skills and also for his single-minded desire for wealth and power.

For a number of years, scouting trips to the Yucatán, in present-day Mexico, had returned with reports of a highly cultured, extremely wealthy civilization. In 1518 Velázquez ap-

pointed Cortés captain-general of a new expedition to explore and conquer the Yucatán.

Velázquez immediately regretted his decision, for he realized if the mission succeeded, the glory would belong to Cortés. Meanwhile Cortés moved very quickly and within a month had assembled eleven ships and six hundred men. Ignoring Velázquez's orders not to sail, Cortés left Santo Domingo as soon as he could and arrived on the coast of Mexico in February 1519.

Above **This map shows Cortés's route to Tenochtitlán, where he overthrew the empire of the Aztecs, and his march back to the Mexican coast, where he defeated Narváez.**

1530
Returns to New Spain; continues his Pacific explorations.

1536
Discovers and explores the Baja California peninsula.

1540
Returns to Spain and retires to his estate near Seville.

1547
Dies in Seville.

Spain in the New World

Cortés lived during the early years of Spanish colonization. When Cortés arrived in Cuba, the Spanish crown awarded him an *encomienda* (grant of land), which included the people living on the land. In return for the right to make the people work for him, Cortés had to protect them and try to convert them to Catholicism.

The system was greatly abused, and native populations in the West Indies declined dramatically in part because of being forced to labor as slaves. In 1542 the Spanish crown adopted the *Leyes Nuevas* (new laws); under these laws *encomenderos* were allowed to extract only tax from the natives, not labor.

Above **La Malinche, Cortés's mistress, acted as interpreter between Cortés and the Aztecs.**

RUMORS OF THE AZTECS

On the coast of southeastern Mexico, Cortés founded the city of Veracruz and had himself appointed chief justice. He encountered and conquered several Mayan tribes and learned that they were united in their hatred and fear of the Aztecs—the famed civilization he had heard about in Cuba—who had imposed a harsh rule over much of Mexico.

Cortés decided to march on Tenochtitlán, the Aztec capital. On learning that some of his men were losing heart and were planning

La Malinche c. 1500–1550

La Malinche was born in about 1500 to a noble Aztec family, and Nahuatl, the Aztec language, was her native tongue. When still young she was sold as a slave to the chief of Tabasco, and while in his service she learned the Mayan language. La Malinche was presented as a gift to Cortés when he conquered the Tabascans.

La Malinche converted to Christianity, changed her name to Doña Marina, and quickly mastered Spanish. Until her arrival, Cortés had communicated with the various native peoples using only clumsy gestures. With La Malinche as an interpreter, he succeeded in uniting several warring tribes in an an alliance against Montezuma and was later able to enter into complex negotiations with the Aztecs. La Malinche soon became Cortés's mistress and bore him a son, Martín.

Although opinion, especially in Mexico, is sharply divided about la Malinche, her defenders claim that without her Cortés would have failed. He would have been unable to negotiate with the Aztecs and may have had to slaughter many thousands more. La Malinche is also praised as the person who helped introduce Christianity and end the human sacrifice and cannibalism that the Aztecs inflicted on the peoples subject to them. Cortés himself wrote in a letter that "after God we owe this conquest of New Spain to Doña Marina."

to return to Cuba, he burned his ships so they could not escape. As Cortés headed toward Tenochtitlán, his leadership skills and vastly superior weaponry won him around six thousand allies, including Totonacs, Tlaxcalans, and Cholulans, all of whom saw him as a potential liberator from the tyranny of the Aztecs.

AZTEC SUPERSTITION

According to an ancient Aztec myth, the white, bearded god Quetzalcoatl would return to reclaim Tenochtitlán during a "one-reed year." According to the Aztec calendar, 1519 was such a year. The Aztec emperor, Montezuma II, had been warned by his prophets of great destruction and havoc. When he heard tales of the pale-faced and bearded Spaniards, with their horses and cannons—neither of which had been seen before by the natives of Mexico—he feared the fulfillment of this prophecy.

THE CONQUEST OF TENOCHTITLÁN

Cortés entered the Aztec capital on November 8, 1519. Montezuma received him with great ceremony and after lengthy negotiations allowed himself to become Cortés's prisoner. The Spanish set about the task of destroying the temples of Tenochtitlán and converting the Aztecs to Christianity.

Meanwhile Velázquez, furious with Cortés for disobeying his orders, sent a force from Cuba under the command of Pánfilo de Narváez to attack him. Cortés was forced to gather his army and march against Narváez. Cortés defeated him and persuaded Narváez's soldiers to join his own army.

Cortés then returned to find Tenochtitlán in chaos. The Aztecs had rebelled, and Cortés was forced to withdraw his men at night. During the *noche triste* (sad night) up to a thousand Spanish soldiers were killed. Montezuma was stoned to death by his own people when he tried to pacify them.

Above **In 1519 Emperor Montezuma II tried to pacify Cortés and his soldiers with gifts of gold, but he could not prevent the Spaniards from entering the splendid Aztec capital.**

Right **Owing to the vast military superiority of Cortés's army, the battle for Tenochtitlán was short and brutal.**

Cortés retreated to Tlaxcala and reorganized his forces. He marched on Tenochtitlán once more in December 1520 and conquered the city street by street. The Aztecs were weakened by European diseases, such as smallpox, caught from the Spanish soldiers, to which they had no immunity. By August 13, 1521, the Aztec Empire had fallen, and Cortés found himself in control of a huge territory that extended from the Pacific to the Caribbean.

The Nahuatl poem excerpted below, an Aztec account of the fall of Tenochtitlán, was written perhaps as early as 1528.

Broken spears lie in the roads;
we have torn our hair in grief.
The houses are roofless now, and their walls
are reddened with blood . . .

We have pounded our hands in despair
against the adobe walls,
for our inheritance, our city, is lost and dead.
The shields of our warriors were its defense,
but they could not save it.

From the "Aztec Lament"

CORTÉS'S LATER YEARS

In 1523 Cortés was named captain-general and governor of New Spain. Tenochtitlán was destroyed, and in its place the construction of Mexico City began. Cortés's independent and reckless behavior, however, made him increasingly unpopular with the Spanish crown, and Velázquez used his influence to turn people against Cortés. After a disastrous expedition to Honduras in 1524, the Spanish sent a commission, under Luis Ponce de Léon, to New Spain to make an official inquiry into Cortés's behavior. When Ponce de Léon died almost immediately, Cortés was accused of murdering him.

Cortés's property was seized and his governorship canceled. While others were given important roles in New Spain, Cortés found himself increasingly ignored. In 1540 he returned to Spain, where he tried to restore his reputation with the king. Cortés died in 1547 in Seville.

SEE ALSO

Cousteau, Jacques-Yves

JACQUES-YVES COUSTEAU (1910–1997) was a pioneering underwater explorer, filmmaker, and environmental campaigner. He was the coinventor of the Aqua-Lung, a device that changed the way divers breathe and move around under water. Through his many books and films, Cousteau revealed the mysteries of life under the surface of the sea.

Born to Swim

Jacques-Yves Cousteau was born on June 11, 1910, in Saint-André-de-Cubzac in southwestern France. When he was ten years old, his father, a lawyer, took a job in New York City, and the Cousteau family relocated. In America Cousteau learned to swim, and in Harvey's Lake in northeastern Vermont, he practiced diving under water while holding his breath.

After two years Cousteau returned to France, where he became interested in films and bought a home-movie camera. In 1930 Cousteau joined the French navy. The navy had its own aircraft, and Cousteau dreamed of becoming a naval pilot. However, in 1936 he had an accident, and his injuries prevented him from becoming a pilot. He was sent to the navy's base at Toulon on the Mediterranean coast, where he swam in the sea every day to regain his strength.

Cousteau the Inventor

Cousteau was fascinated by the fish, the rock formations, and the colors he saw while diving. He held his breath for as long as he could but was frustrated that he was unable to stay under water for longer periods. He knew that to do so would require the invention of a new type of breathing apparatus.

During World War II (1939–1945) Cousteau teamed up with Émile Gagnan, a gas engineer. In 1943 the two men perfected the self-contained underwater breathing apparatus (or scuba), later patented as the Aqua-Lung.

Enabling divers to carry air supplies in cylinders on their back to depths of 330 feet (100 m) or more, the Aqua-Lung revolutionized access to the underwater world.

Below **Jacques Cousteau, the French undersea explorer and oceanographer.**

Above **Cousteau describes the Conshelf projects in 1964.**

In addition to his work on the Aqua-Lung, Cousteau developed an underwater observation vessel, or bathyscaphe. The vessel was a small, highly maneuverable submersible capable of diving to a depth of 1,000 feet (305 m).

EXPLORER AND FILMMAKER
In 1950 Cousteau was given *Calypso*, a former minesweeper that he converted into a research vessel, with cameras capable of filming underwater. He took a period of leave from the French navy, and with a team of divers, he made over a thousand journeys below the surface of the sea. He recorded what he saw, and in 1953 his first book, *The Silent World*, was published. Three years later Cousteau released the film version of *The Silent World*. Audiences were captivated by eighty-seven minutes of color footage of an astonishing undersea world that few had imagined existed.

1910
Cousteau is born at Saint-André-de-Cubzac, France.

1920–1922
Lives in the United States and learns to swim.

1930
Joins the French navy.

1936
Breaks both arms in an automobile accident.

1943
Coinvents the Aqua-Lung (with Émile Gagnan).

1946
Founds the French navy's Undersea Research Group.

1950
Calypso is converted into a research ship.

1952
Cousteau makes the first underwater color film, in the Red Sea.

1953
The Silent World is published.

1956
The film version of *The Silent World* is released; Cousteau leaves the French navy.

1959
Designs a bathyscaphe with Jean Mollard.

1960
Campaigns to stop the dumping of nuclear waste in the Mediterranean Sea.

1962–1965
Directs the Conshelf Saturation Dive program.

Life Underwater

Cousteau left the French navy in 1956 to concentrate on exploring the sea and on campaigning on issues of marine conservation. He was concerned by pollution of the ocean, and in 1960 he led a successful campaign to stop the dumping of nuclear waste in the Mediterranean Sea.

Cousteau longed to spend more time underwater and envisaged a future in which people would live and work under the sea. In the 1960s his Conshelf experiments (Conshelf comes from the words *continental shelf*) tested living conditions underwater. During the 1963 Conshelf II project, five men lived beneath the waters of the Red Sea in considerable comfort for a month.

Cousteau became well-known for his books, films (of which he made more than eighty), and campaigns. During a long life and career Cousteau was the first explorer to reveal the secrets of the undersea world to divers and television audiences. He died on June 25, 1997, aged 87.

Right **Cousteau stands in front of his research vessel, *Calypso,* in Miami, Florida, in 1986.**

SEE ALSO

- Clothing
- Underwater Exploration

1973
Establishes the Cousteau Society.

1977
Receives the United Nations International Environmental Prize.

1985
Receives the Medal of Freedom, America's highest civilian honor.

1997
Dies in Paris, France.

Cousteau describes the first dive he made wearing an Aqua-Lung, in the Mediterranean in June 1943:

A modest canyon opened below, full of green weeds, black sea urchins and small flower-like white algae. The sand sloped down into a clear blue infinity. The sun struck so brightly I had to squint. With my arms hanging at my sides, I kicked the fins languidly and traveled down, gaining speed, watching the beach rolling past. I stopped kicking and the momentum carried me on a fabulous glide. When I stopped I slowly emptied my lungs and held my breath. The diminished volume of my body decreased the lifting force of water and I sank dreamily down. I inhaled a great chestful and retained it. Then I rose towards the surface.

Jacques Cousteau, *The Silent World*

DAMPIER, WILLIAM

WILLIAM DAMPIER (1651–1715) is often credited with being the first Englishman to set foot on Australian soil. Although Dampier spent many years as a privateer (a government-authorized pirate), he was also a pioneer of British scientific exploration of the Pacific, a tradition continued by James Cook and Charles Darwin. Dampier is best remembered for the informative and entertaining journals he kept of his expeditions to South America, Australia, and the Pacific Islands.

Right **William Dampier, the first great explorer-scientist.**

EARLY YEARS

Orphaned at the age of sixteen, William Dampier decided to go to sea. The ship he joined took him first to Newfoundland and then to the Gulf of Mexico. Dampier settled in Jamaica until his early twenties, producing and transporting timber destined for New Spain (present-day Mexico).

From 1679 Dampier took part in a series of buccaneering and privateering expeditions on the Pacific coast of South America. Buccaneering and privateering are forms of piracy, directed against a particular nation—in this case Spain, whose ships were usually loaded with gold. Privateers carried letters of marque, which were special government commissions, whereas buccaneers worked without license of any sort. A fortune could be made from these extremely dangerous pursuits.

A NEW VOYAGE ROUND THE WORLD

In 1683 Dampier set sail from Virginia on a privateering voyage against the Spanish, in a ship commanded by a certain Captain Swan. Eight years later Dampier reached England. His voyage had taken him first to West Africa and then back across the Atlantic and around South America by way of Cape Horn, across the Pacific to the Philippines, and then south to the Spice Islands (the Moluccas), from where the ships finally headed back toward England.

Dampier kept a journal of his travels, which was published in 1697 as *A New Voyage Round the World*. The book became hugely popular. Dampier's adventures make entertaining reading, but his account also contains a wealth of valuable information, including maps of coastlines, charts of currents and tides, observations of indigenous peoples, and studies in natural history.

NEW HOLLAND

In 1699 Dampier was commissioned by the Royal Navy to captain the first British voyage of scientific exploration into the Pacific. The appointment was remarkable—Dampier was,

---

Dampier wrote the following passage as his ship reached the island of Guam (in the Pacific) in 1686:

It was well for Captain Swan that we got sight of it before our provision was spent, of which we had but enough for three days more; for as I was afterwards informed, the men had contrived first to kill Captain Swan and eat him when the victuals was gone, and after him all of us. . . . This made Captain Swan say to me after our arrival in Guam, "Ah! Dampier, you would have made them but a poor Meal;" for I was as lean as the Captain was lusty and fleshy.

William Dampier, *A New Voyage Round the World*

1651
Dampier is born in Somerset, England.

1667
Goes away to sea.

1673
Works on a timber plantation in Jamaica.

1678
Takes part in privateering expeditions in the Caribbean.

1679
Crosses Panama to the Pacific to raid Spanish ships off the coast of Peru.

1683–1691
In a series of privateering expeditions, travels around the world from Virginia to England.

1697
A New Voyage Round the World is published.

1699–1701
As captain of the *Roebuck*, Dampier surveys northwestern coast of Australia. Explores and names New Britain, the Dampier Archipelago, and the Dampier Strait, which separates New Guinea and New Britain.

1703
Is sent on a privateering expedition to Pacific coast of South America; Alexander Selkirk is marooned.

1708–1711
Dampier takes part in a final privateering expedition, this time as pilot, to South America, during which Selkirk is rescued.

1715
Dies penniless in London.

1719
Daniel Defoe publishes *Robinson Crusoe*.

after all, a buccaneer with no experience of naval command, but *A New Voyage Round the World* had won him great fame and admiration as an explorer and observer.

Dampier spent five weeks off the northwestern coast of New Holland (Australia), unimpressed with the lack of freshwater and convinced that Australia was a group of large islands. Heading north from present-day Roebuck Bay, Dampier resupplied in Timor and established that New Guinea and the island he named New Britain were separated by a channel (now called the Dampier Strait). He collected a great many specimens and gave detailed descriptions of the plants and animals he saw. His book about the expedition, *A Voyage to New Holland*, one of the earliest descriptions of Australia and its people, was as popular as his earlier work.

THE *ROEBUCK*

The voyage was beset with difficulties. Soon after leaving London, Dampier fell out with his first lieutenant, George Fisher. Although he had Fisher sent ashore and imprisoned in Brazil, the rowdy crew remained difficult to control, and Dampier's ship, the *Roebuck*, was little more than a leaky and rotting hulk.

From Timor, Dampier and his discontented crew struggled back toward England, stopping to make repairs first at Batavia (present-day Jakarta, Indonesia) and later in South Africa. As the *Roebuck* reached Ascension Island in the South Atlantic in February 1701, the ship sprang a leak, which turned out to be irreparable. The captain and crew were compelled to abandon ship and had to remain on the desolate island until four English ships picked them up in April.

LATER YEARS

The loss of the *Roebuck* and Fisher's complaints led to Dampier being charged with cowardice, drunkenness, and brutality upon return to England. After further privateering, he died penniless in London in 1715.

Alexander Selkirk *1676–1721*

Robinson Crusoe, Daniel Defoe's story of a man marooned on a desert island, was based on the real-life story of Alexander Selkirk. William Dampier was part of the expedition that abandoned Selkirk. He was also a member of the expedition that picked him up.

In 1703 Dampier and Selkirk were part of a privateering expedition along the Pacific coast of South America, under Captain Stradling. In October the ships made for Cape Horn at the tip of South America. Selkirk insisted that his ship was not fit to sail and demanded to be set ashore. Stradling deposited him on the island of Mas-a-Tierra, one of the Juan Fernandez Islands, 400 miles (645 km) from the mainland of Chile. As he watched his ship sail out of sight, Selkirk lost his nerve and called out to be taken back aboard—but it was too late.

For four years and four months Selkirk lived in total isolation. Rats chewed his feet at night, he nearly went mad with loneliness, and the only ship he saw was a Spanish vessel whose crew shot at him. Yet his diet of fruit, vegetables, and goat's meat kept him healthy, and he tamed dozens of cats, who slept with him at night and kept the rats away. His ship sank shortly after leaving him, and most of the crew drowned, so perhaps he made the right decision.

In January 1709 another privateering expedition of two ships, with Dampier this time as pilot, picked up a wild-looking man "cloth'd in Goat-Skins." Dampier remembered Selkirk as a fine sailor and took him on board. They returned to England via the Cape of Good Hope, and thus Selkirk's own voyage around the world was completed.

Selkirk never readjusted to civilization and eventually died at sea in 1721. The essayist Richard Steele noted that the civilized world "could not, with all its enjoyments, restore him to the tranquility of his solitude."

ROBINSON CRUSOË

PARIS — V^{VE} MAGNIN ET FILS, EDITEURS.

Dampier's books remained influential and useful for a long time after his death. Before Dampier exploration had been closely associated with conquest. His books are considered classics, and he is credited with being the first great explorer-scientist.

Above **Daniel Defoe's classic advenure is based on the experiences of Alexander Selkirk, who was set ashore on an island in the Pacific and years later picked up by Dampier.**

SEE ALSO

- Cook, James
- Darwin, Charles
- Tasman, Abel

DARWIN, CHARLES

CHARLES DARWIN (1809–1882) is one of the best-known and most controversial scientists of all time. From 1831 to 1836 he served as naturalist aboard the HMS *Beagle,* whose mission was to explore and map the coast of South America, the Galápagos Islands, and the Pacific coral reefs. His study of the wildlife of this region persuaded him that life on earth had evolved by natural selection. Darwin expounded his theory in two important books, *On the Origin of Species* (1859) and *The Descent of Man* (1871). Darwin's ideas were attacked by, among others, theologians, who considered the theory of evolution to be at odds with the account of the origin of the world given in the Book of Genesis.

Below **This portrait of Charles Darwin was painted in 1840, four years after his voyage on HMS *Beagle*.**

Charles Darwin was born in 1809 to a wealthy family in Shrewsbury (central England). One of his grandfathers was the innovative ceramics manufacturer Josiah Wedgwood; the other was the pioneering scientist Erasmus Darwin.

Charles read theology at Cambridge and was expected to become a minister in the Church of England after graduation. However, during his time at Cambridge, he also pursued his boyhood interest in natural history.

A professor at Cambridge, John Henslow (1796–1861), befriended Darwin and eventually managed to arrange a position for him on board HMS *Beagle*. Henslow admitted that Darwin was not a "finished naturalist," and he suggested that Darwin take plenty of books on the voyage. Darwin's voyage on the *Beagle* changed his life—and the course of nineteenth-century science.

THE VOYAGE OF THE *BEAGLE*

On December 27, 1831, the *Beagle* set sail from Devonport in southwestern England, bound for South America. Only ninety feet (27.4 m) long and twenty-four feet (7.3 m) wide, the *Beagle* carried a crew of seventy-four men, including eight marines to defend the crew in the event of a conflict, an artist to record the expedition, and a technician to repair the ship's navigational instruments. There were also three natives of Tierra del Fuego, taken on board by Captain Robert Fitzroy during his earlier voyage to that place.

The *Beagle's* hold was packed with over six thousand cases of food supplies, barrels of

Above **The *Beagle*, weighing 235 tons (213,192 kg), left Plymouth on December 27, 1831.**

lime juice to prevent scurvy, and preserving fluid for Darwin's biological specimens. Four of the ship's ten guns were taken out to make space for twenty-two chronometers, used by Fitzroy to track the ships longitude. In this cramped space Darwin spent the most influential years of his life, collecting and studying a growing assortment of animals and plants.

The voyage of the *Beagle* took Darwin to the Cape Verde Islands to study volcanic rocks and to the tropical rain forests of Brazil. In Uruguay he found fossils and traveled up the Río de la Plata. He spent time with the native people of Tierra del Fuego, visited the Falkland Islands, and traversed the Strait of Magellan before traveling up the coast of Chile. From here the party made excursions inland to cross the Andes and saw the devastating effects of a major earthquake.

Darwin in the Galápagos

During his exploration of the remote Galápagos Islands in September and October 1835, Darwin collected over two hundred specimens. He marveled at the unusual plants and animals, such as the giant tortoise and the Galápagos iguana. Darwin realized that, although the plants and animals of the Galápagos were similar to those found on the South American continent, many of the Galápagos species were unique to the islands.

Darwin reasoned that, long ago, animals, plant spores, and seeds had been carried six hundred miles across the ocean to the Galápagos from South America. Trapped on the Galápagos, life-forms had gradually evolved (changed over long periods of time) to survive in local conditions. Darwin observed, for example, thirteen similar species of finches, each of which had a bill of a different shape and size. The specialized bill enabled each species to eat different food, and thus the finches avoided coming into direct competition with one another for the limited food supply. The thirteen species of finches were probably descended from a single ancestral species, but each had adapted to the climate and food source of its particular island.

Right **The Galápagos Islands were formed by volcanic action. Some are millions of years old, while Isla Fernandina (shown here) is only about seven thousand years old. The sharp-edged basalt rubble, which geologists call aa, provides a home for many species, including iguanas, sea lions, and seven species of Galápagos lava lizards.**

Darwin had always hoped to be the first European scientist to collect a rare species of ostrich. Halfway through a meal one evening he discovered that he was eating the very animal that he had been looking for. It had been shot by Fitzroy's marines, who often went hunting for fresh meat. Darwin carefully preserved the pieces of the ostrich that had not been eaten by the crew of the *Beagle*. The species is still known as *Rhea darwinii*.

The *Beagle* crossed the Pacific to Tahiti, New Zealand, and Australia before continuing to the Indian Ocean, where, in Mauritius, Darwin studied how coral reefs were formed. The *Beagle* then rounded the Cape of Good Hope, headed for Ascension Island, and finally returned to Falmouth in October 1836. Darwin bought a small estate at Down in Kent and never went overseas again.

A Controversial Idea

During his voyage Darwin filled twenty-four thick notebooks with notes. On returning to Britain he spent years studying his notes and contemplating what he had seen in the Southern Hemisphere. He knew that he had observed natural phenomena that could not be explained according to the principles of traditional biology. He met with local farmers on his estate in Kent, and they told him how they bred animals to promote certain features of the parents in their young.

Darwin's ideas, when he finally published them, provoked a strong response. Christians attacked his views, which contradicted the account of God's creation of the world given in the Old Testament Book of Genesis. Many people were offended by Darwin's idea that man was descended from earlier apelike creatures. Darwin himself said little in public about these controversies. One reason may have been a wish to avoid upsetting his deeply devout wife, Emma.

ILLNESS AND DEATH

While in South America in the 1830s, Darwin had been bitten by an insect carrying Chagas disease, from which he suffered for the rest of his life. The disease contributed to his death in 1882. Charles Darwin was buried with honor in London's Westminster Abbey, close to the grave of Sir Isaac Newton and other highly esteeemed British scientists.

SEE ALSO

• Chronometer • Fitzroy, Robert • Natural Sciences

Darwin's Theory of Evolution

Darwin developed several related ideas into a general theory of evolution. Having seen the lush jungles of South America teeming with life, he knew that many species produce far more young than are needed to replace their population. This situation results in competition for food and for mates. Those creatures best adapted to their environment have the best chance of winning the competition and thus of going on to reproduce—a phenomenon known as survival of the fittest. Their successful characteristics are then passed on to their young, and the species as a whole evolves to suit its environment. Darwin called this process natural selection. Over millions of generations, small adaptations in individual creatures lead to the development of new species. Darwin believed that all life on earth had come about as a result of evolution.

Below **Published in 1859, *On the Origin of Species* changed the way that scientists thought about life on earth. Darwin's ideas are the foundation of modern biology.**

DEAD RECKONING

DEAD RECKONING IS a navigational method based on keeping records of the distance and direction sailed or flown from a known point. For many early explorers, including Christopher Columbus, John and Sebastian Cabot, and Jacques Cartier, dead reckoning was as important as navigation by the sun and stars.

Dead reckoning was developed by European sailors in the Middle Ages. It was made possible by the magnetic compass, a Chinese invention that was in use in the Mediterranean by the twelfth century. Thanks to the compass, whose magnetic needle points north, a navigator always knew the direction in which he was sailing.

CALCULATING A SHIP'S SPEED

To work out the distance traveled, a navigator needed to know his ship's speed over a set period of time. Time was marked with a sandglass, an instrument in which sand falls slowly from one end of a glass to the other. Every half hour, the time the sand took to run through, the glass was turned by one of the ship's boys, who shouted out the time.

Measuring speed was a matter of experience. A good navigator, such as Christopher Columbus, could feel how fast his ship was moving. He might also throw small bits of wood onto the water and watch them disappear behind the ship or observe seaweed or bubbles as they floated past. In the sixteenth century northern Europeans invented the chip log (also called the logline), a more reliable method of measuring speed.

THE TRAVERSE BOARD

The helmsman, the sailor who steered the ship, was also responsible for recording its direction. He either wrote this information on a slate or made marks on a traverse board, a board painted with the face of a compass, with eight holes along each compass point. Every half hour of his four-hour watch, the helmsman put a wooden peg in one of the holes to record the direction he was steering. A second set of holes at the bottom of the board recorded the ship's speed. Later the navigator used the traverse board to determine his ship's position. He multiplied speed by time to give him distance traveled, which he marked on his chart.

PROBLEMS WITH DEAD RECKONING

Much could go wrong with dead reckoning. The navigator had to take account of strong currents and side winds, which might take the ship off its course. There was also the problem of compass variation: early explorers learned that their compass did not always point to true north. In addition, a lazy sailor might sometimes turn the glass before all the sand had run through so that he would have a shorter time on watch, a practice the Spanish called "robbing the glass." Any one of these factors could ruin the dead reckoning.

Modern navigators have sophisticated electronic equipment to help them find their way at sea. Even so, dead reckoning is still a basic navigational technique that every good sailor learns.

c. 250 CE
Compass in use in China.

c. 1180
Compass in use in Europe.

c. 1280
Earliest known European sea chart, the Carte Pisane, showing sailing directions and distances.

1492–1493
Using dead reckoning, Columbus crosses the Atlantic and returns safely home.

The Chip Log

*T*he chip log was a rope with knots tied at equal intervals and a wooden float at one end; the rope was weighted or flanged so that it would not move in the water. A sailor threw the float over the stern and let out the rope for half a minute, timed with a glass. He then pulled in the rope and counted the knots. The number of knots that had played out indicated the ship's speed. Though speed at sea is no longer measured with a knotted rope, the basic unit of speed—one nautical mile per hour—is still known as a knot.

Left **Until the invention of the chronometer in the seventeenth century, navigators measured their ship's longitude by plotting compass direction and speed on a traverse board like this one.**

SEE ALSO

- Columbus, Christopher
- Navigation
- Navigational Instruments

DIAS, BARTOLOMEU

THE PORTUGUESE NAVIGATOR Bartolomeu Dias (c. 1450–1500) became the first European to sail around the southern tip of Africa (1487–1488). With his discovery of the Cape of Good Hope, Dias proved the existence of a navigable sea route from Europe to India and prepared the way for Vasco da Gama's famous voyage ten years later.

Little is known of Bartolomeu Dias's early life, though he may have come from a family of seafarers, as two earlier Portuguese explorers were also named Dias. He was certainly an experienced sea captain who made a number of voyages to West Africa in the 1480s. As well as being the captain of a caravel, the *São Cristóvão*, Dias served the Portuguese king as superintendent of the royal warehouses, the

great buildings in Lisbon where African trade goods were stored.

In 1481 the new king of Portugal, John II, began a deliberate campaign to create an overseas empire. In December 1481 he sent a fleet of nine caravels to West Africa to build a castle at Elmina on the Gold Coast (present-day Ghana) and to begin trading ivory. Dias was one of the captains sailing in the fleet.

Below **Dias sights Africa's southern tip, the Cape of Good Hope.**

Left In 1485, the Portuguese explorer Diogo Cão set up a *padrão* (stone cross) at present-day Cape Cross in Namibia (southwestern Africa). Two years later, Dias passed Cape Cross and became the first European to sail around the Cape of Good Hope at Africa's southern tip. Cão's original cross was taken to the Berlin Oceanographical Museum in 1894; this replica was erected in 1974.

THE SEARCH FOR THE EAST

In the mid-fifteenth century nobody knew the size of Africa or if it was possible to sail around southern Africa and thus reach the Indian Ocean from the Atlantic. In 1482 and again in 1485 King John II sent the explorer Diogo Cão on voyages to follow the African coast. Cão explored 1,500 miles (2,400 km) of new coastline and traveled as far south as present-day Namibia, yet he found no sign of a southern cape. Africa was much bigger than the Portuguese king had expected, but despite this disappointing news, he did not give up hope. In 1486 he ordered Bartolomeu Dias to find the southern cape and the way to India.

1481–1482
Dias sails to West Africa on a trading expedition led by Diogo d'Azambija.

AUGUST 1487
Traces the African coastline to its southern tip.

JANUARY–MARCH 1488
Rounds the southern tip of Africa.

AUGUST 1488
On his return journey sights the Cape of Good Hope.

DECEMBER 1488
Returns to Lisbon.

MARCH 5, 1493
Meets and tries to arrest Christopher Columbus, newly returned from his first Atlantic voyage.

JULY 8, 1497
Accompanies Vasco da Gama on the first part of his voyage to India.

MARCH 8, 1500
Sets sail for India with the fleet of Pedro Álvares Cabral.

APRIL 21, 1500
Cabral reaches Brazil.

MAY 24, 1500
Dias's ship is lost off the Cape of Good Hope.

VOYAGE TO SOUTHERN AFRICA

After ten months of preparation, in August 1487 Dias set off with three ships. Among his supplies were stone crosses (known as *padrões*), each carved with the name of the king and with his royal coat of arms. These crosses would be set up along the coasts to claim the land for Portugal.

Sailing south, Dias's ships passed the last *padrão* left by Cão at Cape Cross, Namibia, and continued south beyond the mouth of the Orange River. Soon after, the fleet was caught in a violent storm that lasted for thirteen days. To avoid being wrecked, the ships kept out of sight of land. Once the weather improved, Dias sailed east, hoping to find the coastline again. After several days without finding land, Dias altered his course to the north and found the coast, which now ran from west to east. He had sailed around Africa's southern tip without realizing he had done so!

Dias erected a *padrão* near the Great Fish River and announced his desire to continue sailing east toward India. However, his men were exhausted and frightened by the recent storm, and they refused to sail any farther. Dias was forced to turn back. It was on his return journey that he sighted the Cape of Good Hope.

LATER VOYAGES

Dias's voyage showed that the way to India was open. Yet it was not until 1497 that the Portuguese took advantage of this knowledge and sent Vasco da Gama's fleet to India. It is not known why there was such a delay. It is possible that in the 1490s the Portuguese were making other unrecorded voyages into the South Atlantic. For when the fleet of da Gama did sail, it took a completely different route from Dias's, sailing far out into the Atlantic. This fact suggests that the Portuguese had learned about the South Atlantic wind system, which blows in a counterclockwise circle.

Dias played an important role in the Vasco da Gama expedition. He oversaw the building of the ships, which were bigger and stronger than those used on the previous expedition and had square rather than triangular sails, a configuration that made the ships faster in the open ocean. He also accompanied da Gama on the first part of his voyage, to the Cape Verde Islands, before leaving the fleet for Elmina.

In 1500 Dias sailed as a captain in the second fleet bound for India, under Pedro

Below **This map shows Dias's route around Africa.**

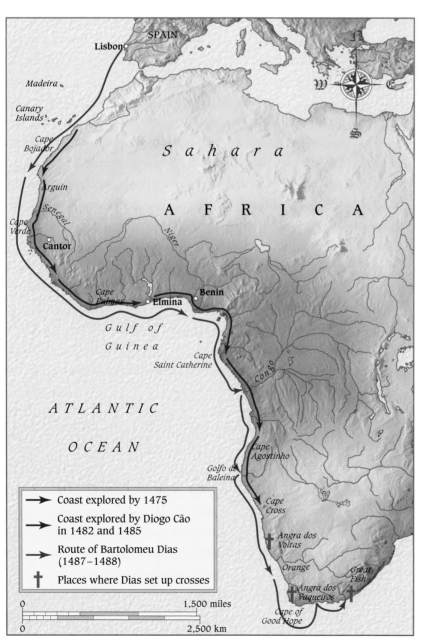

SPAIN

Lisbon

Madeira

Canary Islands

Cape Bojador

Arguin

Senegal

Cape Verde

Cantor

S a h a r a

A F R I C A

Niger

Cape Palmas

Elmina

Benin

Gulf of Guinea

Cape Saint Catherine

Congo

A T L A N T I C

O C E A N

Cape Agostinho

Golfo de Baleina

Cape Cross

Angra dos Voltas

Orange

Great Fish

Angra dos Vaqueiros

Cape of Good Hope

→ Coast explored by 1475

→ Coast explored by Diogo Cão in 1482 and 1485

→ Route of Bartolomeu Dias (1487–1488)

✝ Places where Dias set up crosses

| 0 | 1,500 miles |
| 0 | 2,500 km |

Álvares Cabral. He took part in the European discovery of Brazil, which Cabral found on April 21, 1500. The next month the fleet was hit by a terrible storm off the Cape of Good Hope. Four ships, including that of Dias, were lost with their crews. Thus, Dias died while rounding the very cape that he had found on his famous voyage.

Above **This nineteenth-century engraving shows two of Dias's caravels on their voyage south. Note that the artist has mistakenly drawn covered decks. Caravels were open to the wind and rain.**

In a 1552 book a Portuguese historian describes how the Cape of Good Hope was given its name:

On their return journey, they came at last to the famous cape which had remained undiscovered for so many centuries. . . . Bartolomeu Dias called it the Cape of Storms because of the terrible weather they had experienced there when first rounding it. But when they returned to Portugal, the king gave it the pleasanter name of Cape of Good Hope, for he had good hopes of finding the passage to India beyond it.

João de Barros, *Asia*

SEE ALSO

- Cabral, Pedro Álvares
- Columbus, Christopher
- Gama, Vasco da
- Portugal

DRAKE, FRANCIS

FRANCIS DRAKE (c. 1540–1596) was born in Tavistock in the southwestern English county of Devon. Between 1569 and 1572 he became a wealthy sea captain by attacking Spanish ships in the Caribbean. In 1577 he set out on a voyage around the globe that lasted three years. He also played a significant part in defeating the Spanish attempt to invade England in 1588.

Below **Francis Drake was a brave sea captain, a successful businessman, and a fashionable courtier.**

Francis Drake first sailed to the Americas in 1566 and returned there the following year with his cousin Sir John Hawkins. The two men traded in African slaves with the Spanish colonies in Central America and the West Indies. While there Drake learned of the great wealth that Spain took from the Americas. He returned to the Caribbean in 1569, 1571, and 1572, attacking and looting Spanish ships and trading settlements.

In 1572, with the help of rebel slaves called the Cimaroons, Drake carried out a daring overland journey across Panama to attack the mule trains that carried gold and silver from the mines to the Spanish ships lying off the coast. In Darién he climbed a mountain and looked out over the Pacific; he was the first Englishman to see this vast ocean.

VOYAGE AROUND THE WORLD

In December 1577 Drake left Plymouth with five ships and 160 men. His aim was to explore those parts of South America outside of Spanish control, with a view to future English settlements. Drake also planned to search for the southern continent, as well as an entrance to the Northwest Passage. During the voyage he changed the name of his flagship from *Pelican* to *Golden Hind*.

1565–1567
Drake sails with Sir John Hawkins on slaving expeditions.

1569–1572
Raids Spanish ships and bases in the Caribbean.

1572–1573
Crosses Panama; sees the Pacific Ocean.

1577
Leads voyage of the *Golden Hind* in search of the southern continent.

1578
Sees that Tierra del Fuego is not connected to southern landmass.

1579
Lands at Nova Albion in northern California.

1580
Returns to England and thus completes first British circumnavigation of the world.

1581
Is knighted by Queen Elizabeth I.

1586
Rescues colonists from Roanoke; brings back tobacco and potatoes.

1588
Is appointed vice admiral of the English fleet; helps defeat the Spanish armada.

1596
Dies off Panama coast and is buried at sea.

Left Drake's flagship, formerly the *Pelican*, was renamed the *Golden Hind* in honor of Christopher Hatton, one of Drake's principal backers, whose family crest included a golden hind (a type of deer). The *Golden Hind* was a sound ship that survived fierce storms in the Strait of Magellan as well as a collision with a reef in the seas off Indonesia. It even managed to carry a heavy cargo of twenty-six tons (23,600 kg) of Spanish silver back to England.

During the three-year voyage, Drake made several important geographical discoveries. He found, for instance, that Tierra del Fuego, the small body of land south of the Strait of Magellan, was not connected to South America and also that it was not—as some people had previously thought—part of a great southern continent.

Drake landed to repair the *Golden Hind* at a place he named Nova Albion and sailed up the Pacific coast of the Americas as far north as Vancouver Island. He reached the East Indies within three months and raided Spanish ships in the Philippines. The Spanish were taken completely by surprise, as Drake's

Drake's Secret Ships

*F*rancis Drake used ships for long sea voyages that ranged in size from the 100-ton (91,000 kg) *Pelican* to the 175-ton (170,000 kg) *Bark Bonner*. After his first voyages to the Americas, Drake realized that such large ships were unsuitable for exploring the rivers and coastlines of Central and South America. In 1572 he crossed the Atlantic with three dismantled "secret ships" in the hold. These were pinnaces, fast, one-masted boats that could maneuver in very shallow water. The pinnaces were reassembled in the New World and then used to sail up the Francisco River deep inside Spanish Panama. Thus, Drake and his men were able to surprise and scatter the enemy garrison at the treasure port of Nombre de Dios.

Nova Albion

*I*n the summer of 1579, Francis Drake explored the northwestern coast of North America. On June 17 he recorded in his log that he had discovered "a fit and convenient harbour" at a latitude beyond 38 degrees. His ship anchored there until July 23, although Drake noted that "notwithstanding it was the height of summer, we were continually visited with nipping cold." Drake claimed the surrounding land for Queen Elizabeth I of England and named it Nova Albion (New Britain). A later map from around 1596 by Hondius shows Portus Novae Albionis (Drake's Harbor) in northern California. Modern historians continue to argue about exactly where Drake landed, but many believe that he had discovered San Francisco Bay.

was the first British fleet to reach Asia by the Pacific route.

Drake finally returned to England, via the Cape of Good Hope, on September 26, 1580. He thus became the first English captain to circumnavigate the globe. Queen Elizabeth met him at Deptford, on the Thames River. She later rewarded Drake with a knighthood.

LATER YEARS

In June 1586 Drake was involved in bringing home some of the colonists sent out by Sir Walter Raleigh to Roanoke, Raleigh's failed settlement on the Carolina coast. The settlers brought back from the Americas two plants, at that time unknown in Europe, soon to play very important (although very different) roles. The plants were tobacco and potatoes.

Drake played a major role in frustrating Spain's plan to invade England in 1587. By burning the Spanish fleet and its supplies at Cádiz in spring 1587, he delayed the sailing of the armada (the Spanish naval force) by a year. When the armada eventually sailed in May 1588, Drake helped to destroy it, capturing the flagship *Rosario* in the process.

Having returned to Panama to raid Spanish ships for profit once again, Drake died in January 1596 after a severe attack of dysentery. He was buried there at sea in a sealed lead casket.

Left **Queen Elizabeth invested 1,000 crowns in Drake's sea voyage of 1577 to 1580 and received a profit of 47,000 crowns in return. She rewarded him with a knighthood—conferred on board the *Golden Hind*—in 1581.**

SEE ALSO
- Great Britain • Magellan, Ferdinand
- Northwest Passage • Raleigh, Walter

EARTH

AS RECENTLY AS a few centuries ago, people knew little about the earth. Voyages of exploration have made an immeasurably significant contribution to knowledge of this planet. Scientists may develop theories about the planet, but it is explorers who prove (or disprove) them. For example, flat-earth theories, although not widely held, persisted well into the Middle Ages. Scientists long suspected that the earth was round, but it took explorers to prove that it was—by sailing all the way around it. Although many early journeys of exploration had the primary aim of territorial enlargement—with increased knowledge being an incidental result—the desire for knowledge of the earth for its own sake has been a driving force of a great many modern journeys of exploration.

THE EXPLORATION OF THE EARTH

Early voyages of exploration were launched for various reasons. Most had the aim of conquering new land; some of finding new markets for trade; others of spreading religion. Many individual explorers were also driven by curiosity about what they might find when they reached the edge of the area they knew.

Left **This satellite photograph of the earth, showing the continent of Africa, was taken by the European weather satellite** *Meteosat.*

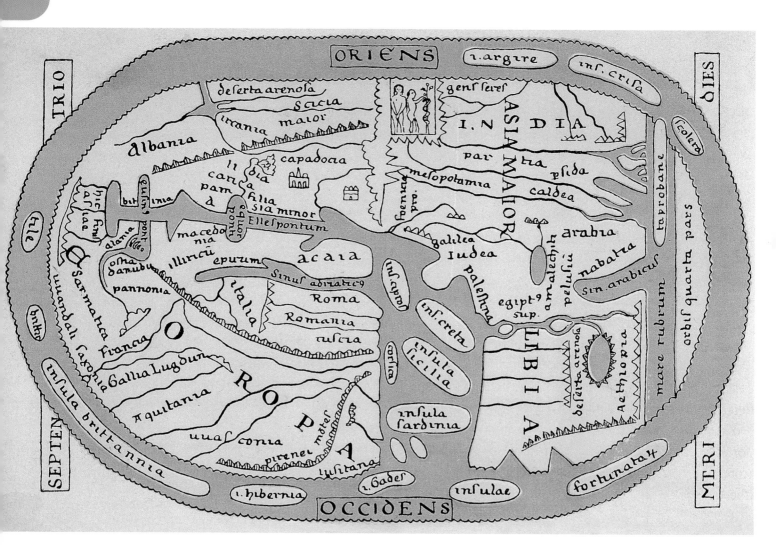

ORIENS

TRIO · DIES · SEPTEN · MERI

OCCIDENS

Above **This map of the world, with east at the top, was drawn in France in 1076 by Stephanus Garcia.**

The history of the exploration of the earth may be divided into three stages. In the first stage much of the Old World (Europe, Asia, and North Africa) was explored. Next came the Age of Discovery, a period when navigators searching for direct sea routes from Europe to China and India discovered the Americas (the New World) and southern Africa. Finally, explorers looked closer at the land that had been discovered and described the earth in increasing detail.

The earth is still being explored. Although the surface has been mapped, there remains much to learn, for example, about the bed of the sea and the part of the planet that lies beneath the surface. Scientists are also eager to discover whether the universe contains other planets, like Earth, that are capable of supporting human life.

MAPPING THE EARTH

The first explorers did not have maps to guide them but often drew their own as they traveled. These maps were useful on the return journey and for people who traveled to the same area in the future. Although early cartographers (mapmakers) used very basic methods for measuring their position, many of the places featured on their maps can still be recognized.

Geographers went on to study the physical features of the earth, such as mountains, valleys, and deserts. Their work provided information that vastly improved the quality of maps. Cartographers now rely on the latest technology to make sure that maps are exact. Both radar technology and photographs taken from satellites have ensured that every part of the earth's surface has been mapped.

BENEATH THE EARTH'S SURFACE

Geologists study what the earth is made of, including what lies beneath the surface. In the past there were many conflicting theories about what was inside the planet. Volcanic eruptions seemed to suggest that the earth was filled with fire. On the other hand, geysers and springs indicated that it was filled with water.

Around the beginning of the twentieth century, surveys of seismic activity (earthquakes and their effects) allowed scientists to study the geological structure of the planet. More recently, techniques such as drilling and radar mapping have improved understanding of the earth's crust. Geologists believe that the crust is very thin compared with the rest of the planet, which is composed of different layers of molten and solid rock. However, until the development of methods for actually exploring the earth's mantle and core, no one can be certain what lies beneath the surface.

Geological information is used in many ways. Seismic activity is monitored in the hope that warnings can be given before earthquakes occur and volcanoes erupt. The construction industry relies on geological information in order to ensure that structures are built on solid ground that will give them strong foundations. Construction engineers also extract materials from the earth for use in their building projects. Mining industries rely on geological surveys to locate the earth's natural resources, such as oil, gas, valuable minerals, ores, and precious stones. Seismic surveys locate the position of such resources before drilling begins.

Earth Statistics

- **Age:** about 4.5 billion years
- **Time it takes to rotate:** 23 hours, 56 minutes, 4 seconds
- **Average speed:** 18.47 miles (29.79 km) per second
- **Time it takes to orbit the sun:** 365.26 days
- **Diameter (across the equator):** 7,927 miles (12,756 km)
- **Diameter (between the polar regions):** 7,900 miles (12,714 km)
- **Angle of tilt:** 23.45°
- **Average surface temperature:** 59° F (15° C)
- **Temperature of core:** about 9,000° F (5,000° C)
- **Surface area covered by oceans:** 70.8 percent
- **Average thickness of the crust:** 20.5 miles (33 km)
- **Approximate thickness of the mantle:** 1,771 miles (2,850 km)
- **Approximate radius of the core:** 2,156 miles (3,470 km)
- **Natural satellite:** the Moon
- **Distance from the Sun:** 93 million miles (150 million km)
- **Lowest point on the earth's surface:** Mariana Trench in the Pacific Ocean, 36,201 feet (11,034 m) below sea level
- **Highest point on the earth's surface:** Mount Everest, 29,035 feet (8,850 m) above sea level
- **Longest river on earth:** Nile River, 4,123 miles (6,650 km)

---

c. 7000 BCE
Trade between Europe and Asia begins.

c. 2500 BCE
Trade between Europe and Africa begins.

c. 2300 BCE
The earliest surviving map is made by the Babylonians.

c. 1580 BCE
Trade between Africa and Asia begins.

c. 1000 CE
The Viking explorer Leif Eiriksson reaches Newfoundland, in North America.

1492
The Italian explorer Christopher Columbus sails to America; though under the impression he had visited Asia, he becomes the first European to bring reports of the New World.

1497
The Portuguese explorer Vasco da Gama makes a sea voyage to India around the southern tip of Africa.

1519–1522
Ferdinand Magellan, a Portuguese navigator, circumnavigates the globe.

16TH CENTURY
The English and Dutch explore the Arctic.

1616–1627
Dutch explorers reach the western coast of Australia.

18TH CENTURY
France becomes one of the first countries to begin a national survey and mapping program.

19TH CENTURY
Antarctica is discovered.

1909
The American explorer Robert Peary reaches the North Pole.

1911
The Norwegian explorer Roald Amundsen reaches the South Pole.

FINDING THE WAY

Early navigators followed coastlines to make sure they were sailing in the right direction. It was much more difficult to navigate in the middle of open sea, where there were no landmarks, so some sailors recorded details of the currents. Navigators also gradually realized that there was a connection between the tides and the phases of the moon. As all of this knowledge was pieced together, navigators were able to find their way more easily.

The magnetic compass, invented by the Chinese, reached the Mediterranean in the twelfth century. A compass told sailors which direction their ship was facing, although not their position. Some of the most renowned explorers, including Columbus, used a magnetic compass and a navigation method called dead reckoning to work out their location. Starting from a known point, the navigator kept a record of the distance and direction sailed. It was a method that took a great deal of skill and experience—and not a little guesswork.

Invented in the eighteenth century, the sextant enabled navigators to measure precisely the position of the sun and the stars above the horizon and thus to calculate a ship's latitude (its position to the north or south of the equator). However, this method did not reveal a ship's longitude, its position to the east or west of a given point. As a consequence, navigators could not be sure exactly where they were.

It was not until John Harrison (1693–1776) invented the chronometer, a very accurate clock that could be used at sea, that a ship's longitude could be properly measured. Once navigators knew both the longitude and the latitude of their ship, they could work out its exact position.

WEATHER AND CLIMATE

Another type of navigation relied on the weather and the climate. Experienced sailors recognized weather patterns and could use their knowledge to work out where they were. For example, wind blowing from one direction might be a different temperature from wind blowing from another.

Alexander von Humboldt (1769–1859) recorded valuable data, such as temperature and barometric pressure, on trips to South America and Russia. The weather maps he produced were of great importance to nineteenth-century explorers. In the twentieth century, satellites greatly advanced the science of meteorology.

EARTH'S PLACE IN THE UNIVERSE

Throughout history astronomers have attempted to describe the universe and how it works. For many hundreds of years, the universe was thought to be geocentric, that is, to have Earth at its center. It was not until the sixteenth century that Nicolaus Copernicus, a Polish priest and astronomer, realized that the earth was part of a heliocentric system of planets—one with the Sun at its center. In

Revolutionary Ideas about Earth

Until the sixteenth century most people had believed the Greek astronomer Ptolemy's theory that the sun and planets revolved around the earth. The Polish astronomer Nicolaus Copernicus (1473–1543) disagreed. After studying the planetary movements, he realized that the earth and the planets revolved around the sun and that the earth rotated every day. However, not all of his ideas were correct. Copernicus also thought that the sun was at the center of the entire universe and that all planets were the same size and orbited in perfect circles. After his death the Italian astronomer Galileo Galilei (1564–1642) developed Copernicus's theories, which were further corrected by the German Johannes Kepler (1571–1630).

1687 the English mathematician Isaac Newton (1642–1727) drew up his laws of motion, which accurately describe the movement of objects on earth and in space. Newton contributed greatly to scientific understanding of the earth's place in the solar system.

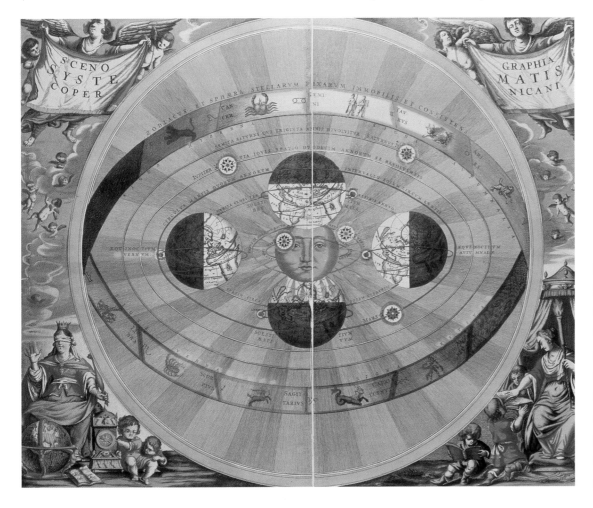

Left **An illustration of the Copernican system, devised by Nicolaus Copernicus, which shows how the earth circles the sun and how the sun illuminates different parts of the globe according to the time of day and the season of the year.**

To the Depths of the Sea

In 1872 the first scientific survey of the sea and the seabed was carried out from the British ship HMS *Challenger*. During a four-year voyage around the world, scientists checked the depth and temperature of the water and the direction of the currents, taking samples from the sea and the seabed as they went. The team aboard HMS *Challenger* was the first to examine deep ocean basins.

The surveys that followed added more detail to the data collected on the *Challenger*. Research vessels capable of drilling into the seabed, submersibles that travel to the ocean depths, and even satellites have been used to explore and map the sea.

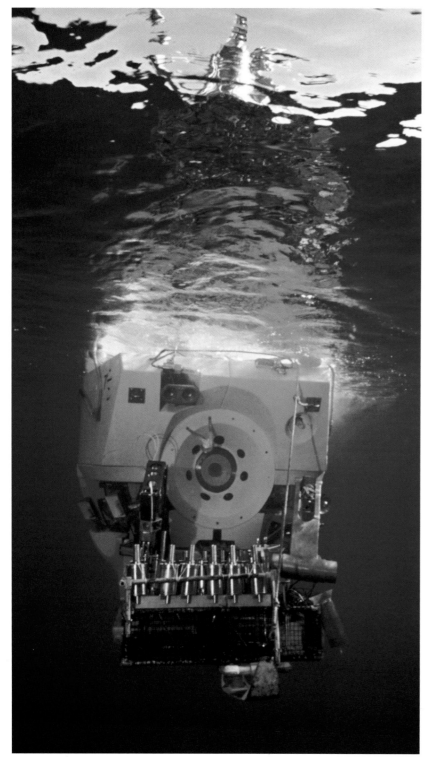

Left **The minisubmarine *Alvin*, pictured here entering the waters off Florida in 1984, has enabled oceanographers to study the depths of the sea.**

Alvin

*A*lvin is a deep submergence vehicle that has been used to explore the depths of the sea since 1964. It operates from the research vessel *Atlantis*. The titanium-hulled submersible can carry three people—a pilot and two scientists—who travel to depths of 13,125 feet (4,000 m) to observe the seabed and deep-sea life. They remain in contact with those on board *Atlantis* at all times via an underwater telephone system. Long movable arms, called manipulators, are used to collect samples, which are placed into a basket attached to the submersible. Also on board are lights, video cameras, computers, temperature probes, and sonar. Two of *Alvin's* most memorable voyages have involved observation of giant tube worms on the Pacific Ocean floor and exploration of the wreck of HMS *Titanic* in the Atlantic Ocean.

SEE ALSO

ELLSWORTH, LINCOLN

THE SON OF A CHICAGO MILLIONAIRE, Lincoln Ellsworth (1880–1951) had a strong sense of adventure that would bring him well-deserved fame. In 1926, along with Roald Amundsen, he led the first expedition to fly over the North Pole, and in 1935 he made the first trans-Antarctic flight.

Lincoln Ellsworth was a surveyor and engineer by profession. During World War I (1914–1918) he joined the American army and trained as an aviator. This experience was to be the start of a lifelong love affair with flying. Ellsworth first made a major mark on the world of exploration in 1924, when he organized a geological survey of the Andes Mountains in South America. What really caught Ellsworth's imagination, however, was the lure of polar exploration. Both the Arctic and Antarctic were vast territories, with thousands of square miles of land that humans had never seen, let alone set foot on.

To follow his dream, Ellsworth teamed up with the experienced Norwegian polar explorer Roald Amundsen (1872–1928). Ellsworth met Amundsen at a low point in Amundsen's life. He lacked funds for further adventures and was convinced his career as an explorer had come to an end. When the wealthy Lincoln Ellsworth introduced himself, Amundsen was delighted to meet him.

FIRST FLIGHT TO THE POLE

Within half a year the Amundsen-Ellsworth Arctic expedition was assembled at Spitsbergen, part of the Svalbard island chain off the northern coast of Norway. Funded by a donation of $85,000 from Ellsworth's father, the men intended to take two German Dornier flying boats named *N-24* and *N-25* to the North Pole.

The planes set off over the vast frozen Arctic Ocean on May 21, 1925. Trouble struck, however, when *N-24*'s engine began to splutter and cut out. Fortunately there was a narrow stretch of open water below them, so both planes were able to land. A brief inspection of the engine showed that *N-24* would not be able to take off again. Then the ice began to close in around the two seaplanes. The Amundsen-Ellsworth Arctic expedition had fallen into an icy trap.

Below **Lincoln Ellsworth as a young man. His rugged good looks and enviable record of achievements made him an American hero.**

Right **Ellsworth photographed in Oslo, Norway, on July 14, 1925, just after returning from his near-fatal first flight to the Arctic with Roald Amundsen. He acknowledges the cheers of people who had turned out to welcome him back to civilization.**

A determined bid to escape followed. For the next twenty-four days the flyers worked twenty-four hours a day, chipping desperately at the ice that threatened to entomb their planes. During this exhausting physical work they had to survive on a mere eight ounces of food per day. On June 15 *N-25*'s engine roared into life, and the pilot made a desperate attempt to lift his overloaded plane into the air. The plane rose up just before it hit the end of the open water and then narrowly managed to clear a twenty-foot (6 m) wall of ice. Near to Spitsbergen, the plane's controls froze up, and *N-25* crashed into the sea. The men were rescued, however, and immediately set about planning a further attempt.

THE *NORGE*

For their next expedition to the North Pole, Ellsworth and Amundsen decided to try using an airship. In the 1920s Italy was producing the world's best airships, so the explorers turned for help to an Italian aviation designer named Umberto Nobile. Ellsworth and Amundsen returned to Spitsbergen in 1926 with Nobile, an Italian crew, and an airship named the *Norge*.

MAY 12, 1880
Ellsworth is born in Chicago, Illinois.

1903–1908
Works as a surveyor and engineer in Canada.

1917–1918
Serves in World War I as an aviator in the U.S. Army.

1924
Leads an expedition to the Andes for Johns Hopkins University.

1925
Flight to North Pole with Roald Amundsen ends in near disaster when their plane is stranded in the ice.

1926
Ellsworth, Amundsen, and Nobile, aboard the airship *Norge*, become the first men to indisputably reach the North Pole.

1931
Ellsworth canoes through Labrador, Canada.

1935
Together with Herbert Hollick-Kenyon, Ellsworth becomes the first man to fly across the Antarctic.

MAY 26, 1951
Dies in New York.

As they made their preparations, they were joined at Spitsbergen by the American flyer Richard E. Byrd and his copilot, Floyd Bennet, who were also planning to fly to the North Pole. Byrd and Bennet took off on May 9 and flew their seaplane over the horizon, returning within the day to announce they had reached the Pole. Although they appeared to have lost the race, Ellsworth, Amundsen, and Nobile decided there was still a record to be had: they would be first by airship.

They set off on May 11 on a flight that was almost without incident. Not only did the *Norge* reach the Pole, it made the first crossing of the entire Arctic Ocean, returning to civilization via Alaska after a 3,390-mile (5,460 km) journey. Despite claims by both Robert E. Peary (on foot) and Byrd (by air), most polar historians agree that Ellsworth and his crew were in fact the first people to reach the North Pole.

The *Norge*

*I*n the 1920s airships were thought to be safer than aircraft, and they could fly for greater distances without the need to refuel. They could also hover, and Ellsworth and Amundsen must have pondered the possibilities of dropping a man onto the Pole via a rope. The *Norge* had a small control cabin, known as a gondola, near its nose. Inside were two lightweight aluminum seats, which Ellsworth and Amundsen commandeered. The rest of the space in the gondola was taken up with packing cases for supplies, and other crew members had to sit on these or stand. Beneath the canvas skin and aluminum skeleton of the airship's huge fuselage were giant gas bags filled with hydrogen, which lifted the craft into the air. Men could enter the airship's vast interior, through a network of ladders and walkways, to tend to these bags and also watch over the petrol engines that drove the *Norge's* three propellers.

Below **This illustration gives a good idea of the size of Umberto Nobile's airship *Norge*, flown from Spitsbergen to Alaska by the Amundsen-Ellsworth expedition in 1926.**

FURTHER ADVENTURES

Ellsworth did not lose his thirst for adventure. In 1931 he canoed 800 miles (1,300 km) through Labrador, on the northeast coast of Canada, and then went on to make pioneering airship flights over the Arctic islands of Franz Josef Land and Novaya Zemlya. The stark beauty of these places appealed to Ellsworth, who spoke of "the gleam of the Northern Lights over the silent snow fields."

In 1935 Ellsworth turned his attention to the Antarctic. He and a Canadian pilot named Herbert Hollick-Kenyon made the first trans-Antarctic flight. Their journey nearly ended in disaster when their plane ran out of fuel and had to land on the ice. However, Ellsworth and Hollick-Kenyon managed to finish their journey on foot.

The Second World War put an end to further polar exploration, and by then Ellsworth was in his sixties. The polar pioneer who made the first trans-Arctic and trans-Antarctic flights died in New York in 1951 at the age of 71.

Right **Aged 56 when this photograph was taken in 1936, Ellsworth (left) poses aboard the rescue ship** *Discovery*, **en route from Antarctica to Australia, with his Canadian copilot, Hollick-Kenyon.**

Umberto Nobile *1885–1978*

Nobile felt he had not received sufficient credit for Ellsworth and Amundsen's triumph of 1926. In 1928 he returned to the Arctic, intending to take his own airship, *Italia*, to the Pole with a crew of sixteen, almost all of them Italians. The trip was a disaster. Ice forming on the airship weighed it down, and the gondola was ripped away from the main body of the airship when it hit the ground. Six men inside the balloon portion of the airship were carried away to their death. Roald Amundsen was one of the many who flew out in search planes to try to save Nobile and his surviving crew. Amundsen's plane crashed, and he was never seen again. The survivors were eventually rescued by a Soviet icebreaker. The disaster was a national humiliation, and Nobile left Italy in disgrace. He later lived in the Soviet Union and the United States before returning to Italy after World War II. He died there in 1978, aged ninety-three.

SEE ALSO

- Amundsen, Roald
- Byrd, Richard E.
- Peary, Robert E.
- Polar Exploration

GLOSSARY

adobe A mixture of silt and clay, dried in the sun, used to make reddish brown bricks for building.

barometer An instrument that measures changes in atmospheric pressure.

barometric pressure A measurement of the pressure of the earth's atmosphere, which changes according to the weather.

bathyscaphe A diving vessel for deep-sea observation, lowered by a cable from a ship.

bends Decompression sickness caused when nitrogen bubbles form in the body's tissues.

buccaneer Name given to English, French, or Dutch sailors who attacked and raided Spanish and Portuguese ships and colonies in the New World.

Cholulan A member of an Indian civilization that flourished around modern Puebla in central Mexico and was probably connected to the Aztecs.

coal-tar naphtha A waste product of the tar-making process.

collier A small ship whose job was to transport coal.

continental shelf The area of the ocean floor closest to land.

doldrums Ocean region near the equator where calms, sudden storms, and light, unpredictable winds predominate.

electromagnetic radiation Energy waves (including visible light, radio waves, and X rays) produced by periodic variations in the electric and magnetic fields of their source. Electromagnetic radiation is dominant on an atomic level but can extend over large distances.

encomienda The medieval Castilian landholding system, involving forced labor and tribute, especially as transferred to New Spain.

fiber-optic cable A cable containing many thin, flexible, transparent fibers, often used to carry telecommunications.

gabardine A smooth, hard-wearing twilled cloth.

hypothermia Dangerously low body temperature caused by prolonged exposure to cold.

mantle The area below the earth's surface and above the core.

Maya A great civilization of southern Mexico, at its height around 800 CE.

meridian An imaginary line, running from the North to the South Pole, used to indicate longitude.

meteorology The study of the weather, especially as a means of forecasting future weather.

Pawnee A member of a Great Plains Indian people that lived in earth lodges along the Platte River, raised crops, and hunted buffalo.

privateer A privately owned ship hired by a government to attack and raid the ships of another country; also, a crew member of such a ship.

radar mapping A procedure for mapping an irregular surface from a distance or through obstacles, such as cloud or ice, by sending out radio waves and analyzing the returning echoes.

seismic Relating to earthquakes or other vibrations of the earth's crust.

sextant An instrument used by seafarers and explorers to measure the height of the sun or a star above the horizon and thus give an estimation of one's latitude.

sonar A system that uses sound waves to detect objects underwater.

Tabascan A member of an Indian people living in an area of southeastern Mexico west of the Yucatán and northwest of Guatemala.

Tlaxcalan A member of an Indian people native to an area of east-central Mexico around Tlaxcala.

topography The physical features of an area, such as mountains, valleys, and streams; also, the study and mapping of such features.

Totonac A member of an Indian people native to an area of east-central Mexico.

ultraviolet A form of short-wavelength radiation.

vulcanized rubber Rubber that has been treated with chemicals at a very high temperature to increase its usefulness.

Wichita A member of an Indian tribe native to the Great Bend area of the Arkansas River in present-day Kansas.

INDEX